MR. GERMAIN GOES TO ANTARCTICA

Stories and Activities to Promote Character Values and Environmental Awareness

By Roxanne Zusmer

Illustrated by John Germain

Roxanne Zusmer
roxannezusmer@gmail.com

Mr. Germain Goes to Antarctica by Roxanne Zusmer — 2nd ed.
ISBN 978-0-9834308-3 4

From past to future, we dedicate this book
to Robert Swan, whose dream became a vision,
and to all those who were a part of
Mission Antarctica and Inspia!,
turning that vision into an everlasting journey
for the world and all humankind.

Seek out the beauty
The awe of Antarctica
Last frontier — pristine

Table of Contents

ACKNOWLEDGMENTS

I wish to acknowledge those who have helped to make the wondrous experience of writing this book more than just a possibility:

John Germain, who allowed me to join him vicariously in his journey to Antarctica, and offered his encouragement and friendship along the way.

The Voyage I team members and crew, whose input added a valuable depth to the stories, and whose interest made me feel a part of their experiences; and Peter Malcolm, team leader, and Andy Dare, *2041* Skipper, who shared their expertise.

Clint Chapman, whose patience and expertise in re-formatting this revised edition is immeasurable.

Rose Kraemer, fourth grade teacher, for piloting this book with her gifted students and sharing its vision with them.

My lifelong friends who have always been there for me through thick and thin.

My family, whose love is priceless and whose strength is endless.

Roxanne Zusmer

I wish to acknowledge those who made my extraordinary journeys to Antarctica and South Africa possible:

Robert Swan, whose vision and friendship will always be a source of light and inspiration to me. Without him, this journey would never have happened.

Citrix Systems and Coca-Cola for their generous sponsorship; the Voyage I crew and team for their patience and comradeship; Peter Malcolm for his expert leadership; Arlene Ortenzo, Principal of Ruth K. Broad Bay Harbor Elementary School for her enthusiastic support; my colleagues and friends for their help and advice; and the entire Germain family for being there.

Roxie Zusmer, whose conception for the book and wonderful writing helped me to revisit the grandeur of the ice.

John Germain

Penguins, seals, whales, birds
Invite you to share the awe
That's Antarctica

FOREWARD

My dream began at age eleven with my fascination for the true polar heroes like Scott and Amundsen and their incredible journeys to Antarctica. This became my life's mission and by May, 1989, I was the first person to walk to both the North and South Poles. At the time, our team's problem was just to stay alive, but all around us the world was changing. We realized we needed to do something about it.

People feel powerless faced with the immensity of global environmental issues. They are swamped under a deluge of information, but there is a critical shortage of inspiration. I decided it was my mission to help inspire others to make a difference.

Maintaining a positive view — embarking on a global mission and inspiring people — was the challenge United Nations World leaders at the Rio Summit in 1992 presented to me. That's how Mission Antarctica was born. By the next World Summit on Sustainable Development in Johannesburg in 2002, a decade later — after a titanic struggle in the worst conditions on earth — we reported back to the world that we had cleared over 1,000 tons of solid waste from Antarctica and recycled it in Uruguay.

There is a critical shortage of leadership. We need positive role models, people who can lead by example. The key to the future is sustainability. That journey is possible when we take small, achievable steps. *Mr. Germain Goes To Antarctica* is a book that inspires our children and adolescents to take that small, first step. Indeed, our youth are the hope of the planet's future. The multiple threats of global warming, urban pollution, war, and AIDS are calls for action. This book is such an action. By aiming to educate our youth on environmental and social issues, and build strong character, we are striving toward producing adults who hold environmental stewardship and inspirational leadership as priorities.

Robert Swan, O.B.E.

Capture the moment
Recognize its potential
Then make it your own

INTRODUCTION

THE BOOK

Mr. Germain Goes To Antarctica is a book that inspires environmental awareness and character education. The stories and activities are based on John Germain's journal as a team member of the Mission Antarctica Voyage I expedition, December, 2001 - January, 2002.

The author, Roxanne Zusmer, and illustrator, John Germain, have worked in a collaborative effort to bring an important message to our children and adolescents about how they can each make a difference, not only in the world as it is today, but as it will be for generations to come. *Mr. Germain Goes To Antarctica* is not only a story, but a meaningful, inspirational learning experience. All readers, including parents, teachers, and counseling professionals are provided with information, activities, and resources that embrace a wide-ranging scope of the curriculum including reading, language arts, social studies, social skills and self-awareness.

True fascination
An 11-year-old's dream
Reach out and explore

ROBERT SWAN, O.B.E.

Robert Swan, O.B.E. (Order of the British Empire), an explorer and environmentalist, is the first man ever to walk unsupported to both the North and South Poles. In 1986, along with Roger Mear and Gareth Wood, he arrived at the South Pole after traveling 883 miles without radios or assistance of any kind. For this accomplishment, he was awarded the Polar Medal by Queen Elizabeth II of Great Britain. In 1989, Robert successfully reached the North Pole, and so became the first person to have walked to both Poles.

In 1992, as keynote speaker at the Rio Earth Summit, Robert presented a universal message: *"that it is possible to achieve your goals and fulfill your ambitions in both your personal and professional life."* It was at this Summit that Robert was chosen by the United Nations and a number of the world leaders to design a decisive, positive action that would inspire young people and involve industry and business. His contribution to education and the environment have been recognized through his appointment as UN Goodwill Ambassador for Youth and a Visiting Professorship in the School of Environment at Leeds University, in England. In 1994, he became Special Envoy to the Director General of UNESCO.

In 1996-97, Robert organized the One Step Beyond, the South Pole Challenge expedition where he led 35 young explorers from 25 nations to Antarctica. These "Special Junior Envoys" joined in assisting the Russians at the Bellingshausen Station with the removal of over a thousand tons of waste from a formerly unspoiled Antarctica.

Robert speaks all over the world on motivational leadership and teamwork. He remains steadfast in his commitment to involve young people and businesses in a dedicated effort toward the preservation of the Antarctic Wilderness as a pristine environment, and an awareness of global climate change. He is hopeful that his message will inspire others to take small achievable steps of environmental and sustainable action.

Bibliography:

www.yahoo.com (Search: Robert Swan)

#1 Home

#4 *Earthship: Mission Possible*

Not just a voyage
An inspirational journey
Making a difference

MISSION ANTARCTICA

THE STORY

This is a story not just of a yacht's voyage, but of an inspirational journey of people in action, action that will make a lasting difference. It is the story about the vision of a man, Robert Swan, and an international effort of commitment to the preservation of the last wilderness, Antarctica, the coldest, windiest, highest, and driest continent on earth.

In the year 2041, the Antarctic Treaty expires. The treaty states that Antarctica may be used only for peaceful, scientific, and educational purposes. Forty-four nations are part of the Antarctic Treaty. Antarctica is owned by no one. It is the aim of Mission Antarctica that we preserve Antarctica for future generations and share knowledge about the largely unknown continent.

The story actually began in 1994 with the One Step Beyond expedition of 35 young people from nations around the world who fostered aims of peace and promotion of international understanding. Their voyage led to the realization that young people in the future must never forget these aims. The question was how to accomplish this task. The answer lay in the tons of waste and rubbish that people had left over the years in Antarctica. And so Mission Antarctica was born.

The first global initiative of Mission Antarctica, one of hope and collaboration, was to assist the Russians in clearing 1,000 tons of rubbish from their scientific research station at Bellingshausen. At this station, located on the southeastern end of King George Island on the Antarctic Peninsula, buildings and machinery had been left to rust and rot over the years. Bellingshausen, which lies 600 miles from civilization, is on a rocky beach that for nine months of the year is completely inaccessible, locked in by ice. Scrap materials that were scattered all over the difficult terrain had to first be collected before a ship could be chartered to remove the waste. This task, which took several years, was accomplished by a Russian and British team of engineers and workers, an effort that was paid for by Mission Antarctica.

Character values
Environment awareness
Both are essential

MISSION ANTARCTICA'S EDUCATIONAL VOYAGES

Robert Swan raised the funds for five Mission Antarctica voyages through sponsor companies interested in supporting the aim of environmental and educational effort on the continent of Antarctica. The yacht *2041* not only added an element of adventure in reaching out to the world with its commitment, but also gave educators and students the possibility of seeing for themselves the cleanup efforts being carried out at Bellingshausen through a series of five educational voyages.

Students and teachers were chosen for these Mission Antarctica voyages through written application and recommendations from school principals. They were asked to complete a 1,500 word essay on: *"How will you apply your experience in Antarctica to further support and implement Mission Antarctica's aim of preserving Antarctica for future generations, and ensure that Antarctica continues to be used only for peaceful scientific and educational purposes? How will you help to spread the Mission Antarctica story throughout the global community, in particular your own country?"*

The waste removal operation completed a four-year commitment by Mission Antarctica, with the bulk of the waste, which was metal, being taken by a freighter, *Anne Boye*, to Uruguay, and the oils returned to the UK for recycling and safe disposal. There are still tons of waste in Antarctica, most of it generated by scientific research stations there. Since Mission Antarctica began its efforts to clean up Antarctica, American, British and Australian bases have committed to the removal of waste from their own research stations.

In 2002, Mission Antarctica linked with loveLife, an organization devoted to educating the disadvantaged youth of South Africa about HIV/AIDS. Mission Antarctica has focused on the stewardship of the environment with the belief that without a clean world and a sustainable way of living, we are endangering ourselves as residents of the planet. loveLife is focused on the lifestyle of the individual as it relates to AIDS which has devastated, and continues to devastate, the population of South Africa. There is no sustainable future for South Africa if its citizens continue to contract the HIV virus. Mission Antarctica and loveLife have joined forces toward safeguarding the individual and the environment in which he or she lives.

Mission Antarctica's Voyage IV team included six South African students, loveLife groundBreakers, who provided inspiration to their fellow youth in their long-term campaign against AIDS. Mission Antarctica and loveLife maintain that through education and effort we are able to affect our lives and the environment in which we live through positive action. In the words of Robert Swan, *"We need leadership by example, new ways of thinking and working together to inspire people to believe that they can make a difference through small, achievable steps."*

John Germain, an art teacher at Ruth K. Broad Bay Harbor K-8 Center, Bay Harbor Islands, Miami-Dade County, Florida, was one of four teachers and four students chosen for Voyage I from more than ninety participating countries, and was the only representative from the United States. The other educators and students were from Fiji, Slovenia, Lebanon, Great Britain, New Zealand, and Australia. Sponsored by Citrix Systems, John Germain brought to realization his commitment to *"raise the consciousness of young people on the role that Antarctica plays in preserving our environment."* His voyage to the frozen wilderness took place from December 30, 2001 through January 15, 2002.

Mr. Germain Goes To Antarctica was written in collaboration between John Germain and Roxanne Zusmer, formerly a school counselor at Ruth K. Broad Bay Harbor K-8 Center. Their aim was twofold: to clarify the goals of Mission Antarctica, and to instill the character values that are depicted through the stories of people and events on Mission Antarctica's Voyage I.

Bibliography:
2041 - The Voyage South, Mission Antarctica Yacht and Expeditions and 2nd Nature Ltd.
Mission Antarctica's Educational Voyages with Teachers and Students, Jan - Mar 2002, Report by Project Manager: Peter Malcolm, 15/2/02

www.inspia.org

VOYAGE I – CHARACTER SKETCHES

Teachers, Students, and Crew

Imagine meeting someone for the first time. Now, imagine meeting seven people at the same time. Expand on that thought and imagine that those seven people were from different countries and cultures throughout the world. Finally, imagine living on a sixty-seven-foot yacht for ten days with those seven people who were, in fact, strangers to each other. Add four crew members and an expedition leader from various countries and you have an interesting picture!

Let's take a look at these new adventurous teammates and the crew who had to learn to live and work together throughout their Mission Antarctica journey:

All of the following four students were excited and grateful to have been a part of Mission Antarctica. They chatted and exchanged interests, hobbies, likes, and dislikes as teenagers might do. All four girls got along well with each other during the Voyage I journey:

Ghia, a smart, charming Lebanese girl, was born in the United States but grew up in Lebanon, a country in southwest Asia. She described the rebuilding of war-torn Beirut, the capital city of Lebanon. She described how far that city has come in the rebuilding process.

Katja, a bright, pleasant girl from Slovenia, a small country in central Europe, showed much enthusiasm about helping to keep Antarctica as an undestroyed part of the earth. She felt that everyone should work together toward this goal.

Mere, a tall, intelligent, polite dark-skinned girl was from Fiji, a country on a group of islands in the southwest Pacific. She carried herself with a quiet, regal posture. She talked about her country's burdens resulting from military actions.

Kaewyn, a slender, good-natured blond girl from New Zealand, was a student who enjoyed speaking of her family back home. She offered a lot of information about her homeland and talked about the World Cup Challenger Races.

The following teachers on Voyage I worked and lived together in harmony, enjoying each other's interests and stories. Factual Misja, down-to-earth Macs, and creative thinkers Nick and Mr. Germain were a good balance in personalities:

Misja (pronounced Mee-sha), a very likable, blond science and physics teacher from the Netherlands, always took a scientific approach to everything, paying a lot of attention to detail. Married, with two children, he has been teaching at a high school in Melbourne, Australia.

Nick, an art teacher from England, is a thin, easygoing, and enthusiastic man. He and Mr. Germain had some fulfilling conversations about art education for young children since they both have been teaching elementary school students. He is married with two children.

Sharon, whose nickname is Macs because of her last name, McNamara, is a friendly, down-to-earth teacher who loves the outdoors. Her actual title is educational outreach coordinator. She met Robert Swan, the coordinator of Mission Antarctica, after a World Wildlife Fund meeting.

Mr. Germain, whose first name is John, is the main character in the stories in this book. (Throughout the book, he is referred to as "Mr. Germain.") He was honored to be representing the United States on this exciting expedition to Antarctica. Mr. Germain is an artist, as well as an art teacher at the New World School of the Arts.

The following four crew members, who were all British, pursued sailors' lives from early ages:

Andy was the captain (or skipper, as he was called) of the yacht *2041*. A highly skilled sailor, he was a commanding figure, decisive and strong. It was Andy who had the responsibility of the expedition's course, as well as the safety of all team members and crew on the yacht. An expert at racing, Andy has sailed in World Cup competitions.

Alexandra (who is called Alex) was the first mate of the yacht. She was competent, considerate of others, and helpful, as well as a highly qualified teacher of sailing skills. She warmed up to the Voyage I team members and displayed a sense of humor. It was Alex who handled, in a calming manner, any potential problems between skipper Andy and others.

Alf, the second mate of the yacht, was strong and silent, a true picture of a rough-and-tumble sailor, willing to do the tough jobs and tasks that required simple hard work. He put the harmony of the crew above any personal gripes he might have had with anyone, never outwardly displaying any feelings of disagreement.

Mike, the engineer of the yacht, was the jester of the group ... comical, playful, and mischievous. He was highly intelligent in all matters dealing with mechanics, engineering, or fixing anything that was broken. He and Alf were the comedy team of the group. Their trouble with the motor for the dinghy was an ongoing joke during the entire expedition.

Peter, who is from Australia, was the expedition leader of Mission Antarctica's Voyage I. He has known Robert Swan since their school days and was a part of Robert Swan's walk to the South Pole. Peter has been involved in environmental causes over the years, making certain his voice was heard. He is a fascinating storyteller whose knowledge of various cultures and wildlife is far-reaching and detailed.

All of the crew members, as well as Peter, the expedition leader, were very aware of their responsibilities for the safety of the group. Mr. Germain felt they were on the lookout for anything that would endanger their lives or well-being, both aboard the *2041* and on land. The Voyage I team members are grateful for all of their expertise and care.

VOYAGE I TEAM / POINTS OF ORIGIN

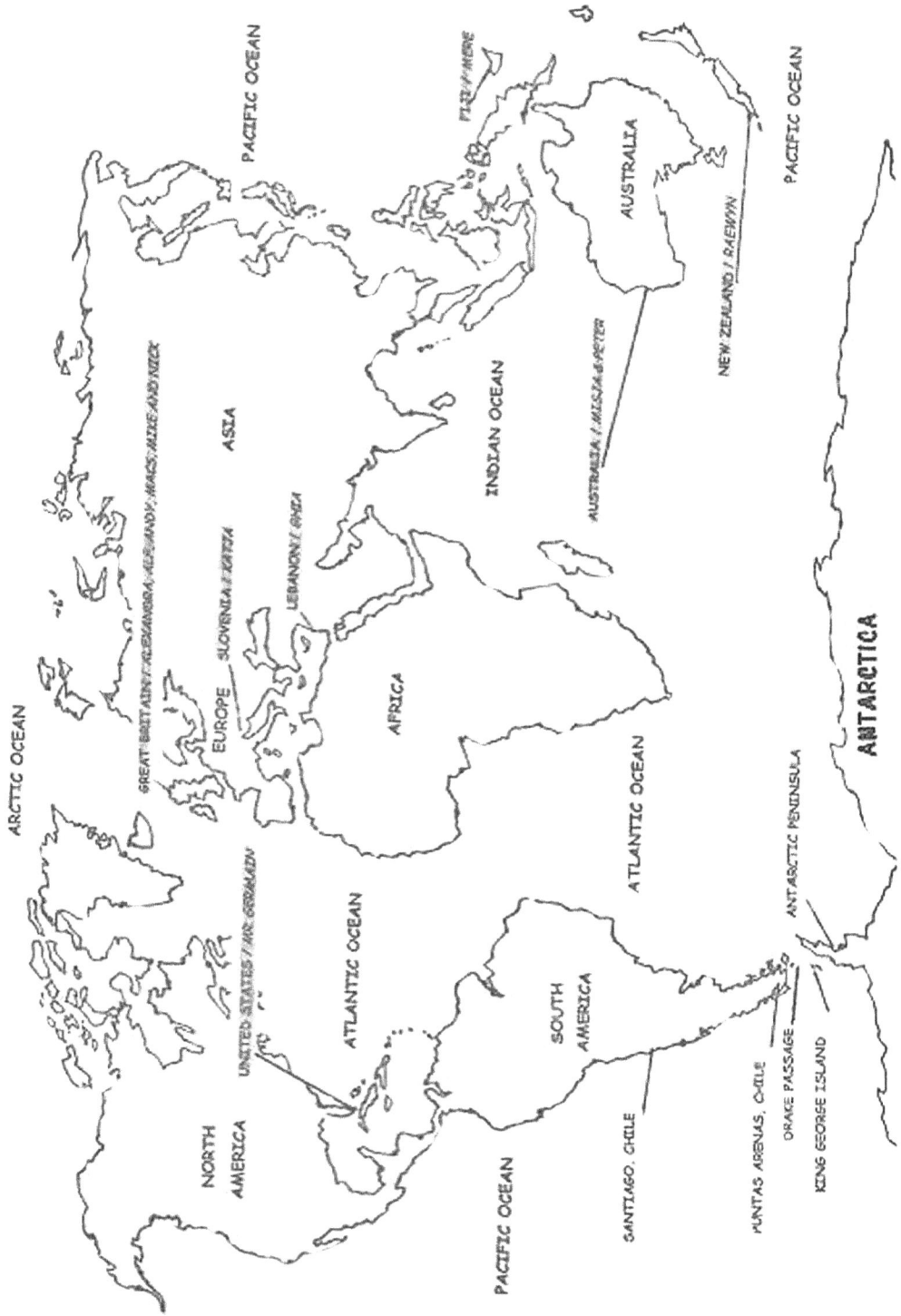

HOW TO USE THIS BOOK

Overview of Introduction

The Book describes the meaning and purpose of the text; explains how the introduction is divided into segments; and provides a brief overview of the scope of curriculum it embraces, including reading, language arts, social studies, social skills, and self-awareness. It promotes the environmental awareness and character education that are essential components of *Mr. Germain Goes to Antarctica*.

Robert Swan, O.B.E., tells of an eleven-year-old boy's dream and how it became a reality when he became a man. Determination and perseverance are character values that will help young people fulfill their own dreams and turn these dreams into their own realities. Through reading about Robert Swan and his accomplishments and commitment to the environment, readers will be able to development a sense of leadership and team building as they review their own attitude and outlook toward the environment in which they live.

Mission Antarctica: The Story describes an inspirational journey and an international effort of commitment to the preservation of Antarctica. It offers readers a clearer picture of the global initiative of Mission Antarctica, including its purpose and vision.

Mission Antarctica's Educational Voyages relates how a series of five educational voyages were conceived. Readers will learn of the collaborative efforts of explorers, environmentalists, and businesses that gave teachers and high school international baccalaureate students the opportunity to take part in, and see for themselves, the dynamic efforts at cleaning up the debris and waste at Bellingshausen, King George Island, Antarctica. It is a learning experience for readers involving forms and applications, environmental awareness, and teamwork and cooperation among nations. It also shows how this book came to be through the participation of John Germain on Voyage I, the first of five voyages to Antarctica.

Voyage I - Character Sketches helps students grasp a clearer image of the students, teachers, and crew who lived and worked together on Voyage I. The first names of the team members, crew, and expedition leader are their actual names. Since the book is entitled *Mr. Germain Goes to Antarctica*, John Germain is referred to as Mr. Germain throughout the stories in the book. It is interesting for the readers to note the various countries that are represented in this international effort.

Overview of Chapters

There are sixteen chapters in this book. In each chapter you will find the following format:

Character Values: Character education is a valuable part of developing the whole person. Each chapter is "announced" with two character values. Readers may ask themselves the following questions: How are these character values depicted in the stories? How do they see these values as important in their own lives? Readers may also cite examples from their own experiences.

Vocabulary Words: The vocabulary words are taken from the story in each chapter and are presented in the order in which they occur. In this way, readers are able to gain a better understanding of the words in the context in which they are used. Besides learning the meanings of the words, readers may strengthen their knowledge by alphabetizing the words, circling the words in the story, using the words in sentences of their own, and/or discovering synonyms or antonyms for some of the words. (Teachers and counselors may supplement ideas of their own in working with students on any of the areas of the book.)

Stories: The sequential stories in this book are based on the journal of John Germain's true-life experiences on Mission Antarctica's Voyage I expedition to Antarctica. Anecdotes are also gathered from input from other team members and crew to enhance the stories of the Voyage I adventure. It is ironic that this story actually begins in a blizzard in Mr. Germain's home-town, Buffalo, New York, showing how close Mr. Germain came to missing out on the journey to Antarctica. The stories, which contain factual information, adventures, and humor are written to clarify the goals of Mission Antarctica and instill character values through the characters and events.

Discussion Questions: The discussion questions focus on the stories and character values presented in each chapter. Readers may go back to the stories to find their answers and gain deeper insight into some of the questions.

Thought Question: Thought-provoking questions have been developed to help readers grow in personal awareness. There are no right or wrong answers. Readers may share their thoughts with a friend or family member.

Map Study: Map studies are included only in the chapters where they are applicable. These sections are incorporated to expand the readers' knowledge of the locations of various cities and countries.

Vocabulary Match-Up: All of the chapters include a vocabulary match-up based on the vocabulary words in that chapter. These pages may be used to enhance the readers' understanding of the vocabulary words.

Activity Pages: Each chapter has two or more activity pages. These are based on the story and character values found in each chapter. (The activities may be altered by a teacher or counselor to meet the needs of their students.)

Glossary: There is a glossary at the end of each chapter with the definitions of the vocabulary words in that chapter. The words are listed in the order in which they occur in the story. Readers may use the glossary to learn the meanings to the words and enhance their vocabulary.

Epilogue

The Voyage I expedition has come full circle, and now the team members are required to honor their sponsorships and commitment to Mission Antarctica by carrying through with their action plans. The epilogue takes us from the ending of Voyage I through the World Summit on Sustainable Development in Johannesburg, South Africa, in August 2002, and into visions of the future through the World Summit in Paris, France in 2015. Readers may use the epilogue as a resource guide in strengthening their commitment to "Think Global — Act Local."

Appendix

Appendix A: Answer Keys (for activity pages)

Appendix B: Map of the Voyage I Route of *2041* (gives a clear picture of the route of the yacht *2041*, and helps students gain a better perspective of the islands and surrounding areas)

Appendix C: Mission Antarctica/Inspia! Timeline (1986 - 2016)

Appendix D: Krill: The Antarctic Food Chain (explains the importance of krill in the Antarctic food chain and the effects of global warming on the food chain)

Appendix E: Recommended Reading/Websites (for children/adolescents and adults)

In the words of Robert Swan, *"We need leadership by example, new ways of thinking and working together to inspire people to believe they can make a difference through small, achievable steps."* It is our hope that our children and adolescent youth will be inspired by the stories and activities in this book to make a difference, in their own ways, through their own small, achievable steps.

You are never given a wish without also being given the power to make it true; you may have to work for it, however.

— *Richard Bach*

Perseverance and Problem Solving

VOCABULARY WORDS:

perseverance	considerably
problem-solving	temporarily
snowdrift	frantic
expedition	snowbound
stranded	back roads
maintenance	diesel fumes
de-iced	permeated
feat	shuttle
blizzard	companions

SNOWBOUND!

Oh, my goodness! Mr. Germain was stuck in a snowdrift in ice-cold Buffalo, New York! How could that have happened?! Well, let's start at the beginning ...

It was the end of December, and Mr. Germain had gone to ice-cold Buffalo, New York, to visit his family for the holidays. The days had passed quickly, and it was time to go back to sunny, warm Miami, Florida, where he worked as an art teacher in one of the K-8 Centers. It was especially important to get home because he was due to leave two days later on a special expedition to Antarctica.

At the Buffalo, airport Mr. Germain looked out of the airplane window and watched as the snow kept falling. As the warm water from the lakes caused more snow to fall, he was afraid that the plane would not be able to take off. He was worried about being stranded by Buffalo's worst snowstorm in history. Five minutes before flight time, as the maintenance men de-iced the plane, Mr. Germain watched the baggage being taken off the plane. It was then that the passengers were told that the airport was being shut down and that all flights were being cancelled.

Mr. Germain got off the plane, picked up his luggage at the baggage claim area, and ran for the nearest pay phone to call his sister, Cathy, who lived nearby. He told her that he *had* to get out of Buffalo so that he could find a flight to Miami at an airport in another city. Cathy told him she would pick him up and deliver him to the downtown bus station. This was no small feat since the blizzard had picked up snow and speed considerably. Driving in bumper-to-bumper traffic on the New York State Thruway, Cathy was temporarily blinded by the snow and ran the car into a snowdrift. That's how a frantic Mr. Germain found himself caught in a snowdrift in a blinding snowstorm!

Cathy and Mr. Germain worked together by steering and pushing the car out of the snowdrift back onto the road. Finally, *finally* they reached the bus station, crowded with people who were in the same situation trying to get out of the snowbound city. They discovered that a bus was ready to leave for New York City at any moment. Rushing, Mr. Germain managed to get on the bus at the last minute. Later, he found out that he had gotten on the very last bus that was allowed to leave Buffalo. He arrived in New York City, by way of back roads, nine hours later, smelling like the diesel fumes that had permeated the bus.

Mr. Germain called a friend in New York City who luckily was at home. Staying with his friend, he slept for four hours, waking at 5:00 a.m., and then took a cab to the New York airport where a shuttle plane took him to Miami with one stop in Tampa ... nineteen hours later ... home at last! A tired Mr. Germain was happy that he would be able to make his connection from Miami to Santiago, Chile, where he would be meeting his companions on the way to Antarctica.

Perseverance and Problem Solving

DISCUSSION QUESTIONS:

1. Who was Mr. Germain and where was he going?
2. What problems did Mr. Germain have to resolve to get to where he was going?
3. Describe how Mr. Germain used perseverance in resolving his problems.
4. How did cooperation help in resolving problems?
5. How do you think Mr. Germain felt when he
   a. found out the plane was not going to leave Buffalo and that the airport was being shut down?
   b. discovered that his sister, Cathy, would take him to the downtown bus station?
   c. found himself caught in a snowdrift in a snowstorm?
   d. slept for only four hours at a friend's home in New York City?
   e. was finally able to get home to Miami in time to leave for the expedition to Antarctica?

THOUGHT QUESTION!

Have you ever been in a similar situation where you had difficulty getting to where you needed to be?

ACTIVITIES:

MAP STUDY
Find the following locations on a map:

- Buffalo, New York
- New York City, New York
- Miami, Florida
- Tampa, Florida
- Santiago, Chile
- Antarctica

VOCABULARY MATCH-UP
Match the vocabulary words with their definitions.   *(See activity page.)*

MAZE
Help Mr. Germain get from Buffalo, New York to his home in Miami, Florida.
(See activity page.)

SEQUENCE OF EVENTS
Number these scenes in the order in which they occurred.   *(See activity page.)*

Perseverance and Problem Solving

VOCABULARY MATCH-UP

MATCH THE VOCABULARY WORDS WITH THEIR DEFINITIONS

Vocabulary Words

_____ perseverance	_____ considerably
_____ problem-solving	_____ temporarily
_____ snowdrift	_____ frantic
_____ expedition	_____ snowbound
_____ stranded	_____ back roads
_____ maintenance	_____ diesel fumes
_____ de-iced	_____ permeated
_____ feat	_____ shuttle
_____ blizzard	_____ companions

Definitions

A. trip for a specific, or special, purpose

B. storm with heavy snow, strong winds, and bitter cold

C. continued effort in spite of difficulties

D. spread through an area

E. streets off the main roads

F. for a limited time, or not permanent

G. smoke or vapor from fuel used to operate a bus engine

H. finding the way out of a difficulty, or finding a solution

I. prevented or removed ice formations

J. wild with excitement, fear, or anxiety

K. heap of snow piled up by the wind

L. shut in, or closed in, by snow, or not able to get out because of snow

M. keeping in a desirable or working condition

N. an act of achievement, usually showing courage, skill, strength, etc.

O. people who share the work, play, or interests of others

P. left in a helpless position

Q. a great amount or extent

R. plane, train, etc. that makes short trips back and forth between two places

Perseverance and Problem Solving

MAZE

BUFFALO

Help Mr. Germain get from Buffalo, New York to his home in Miami, Florida before he misses his flight

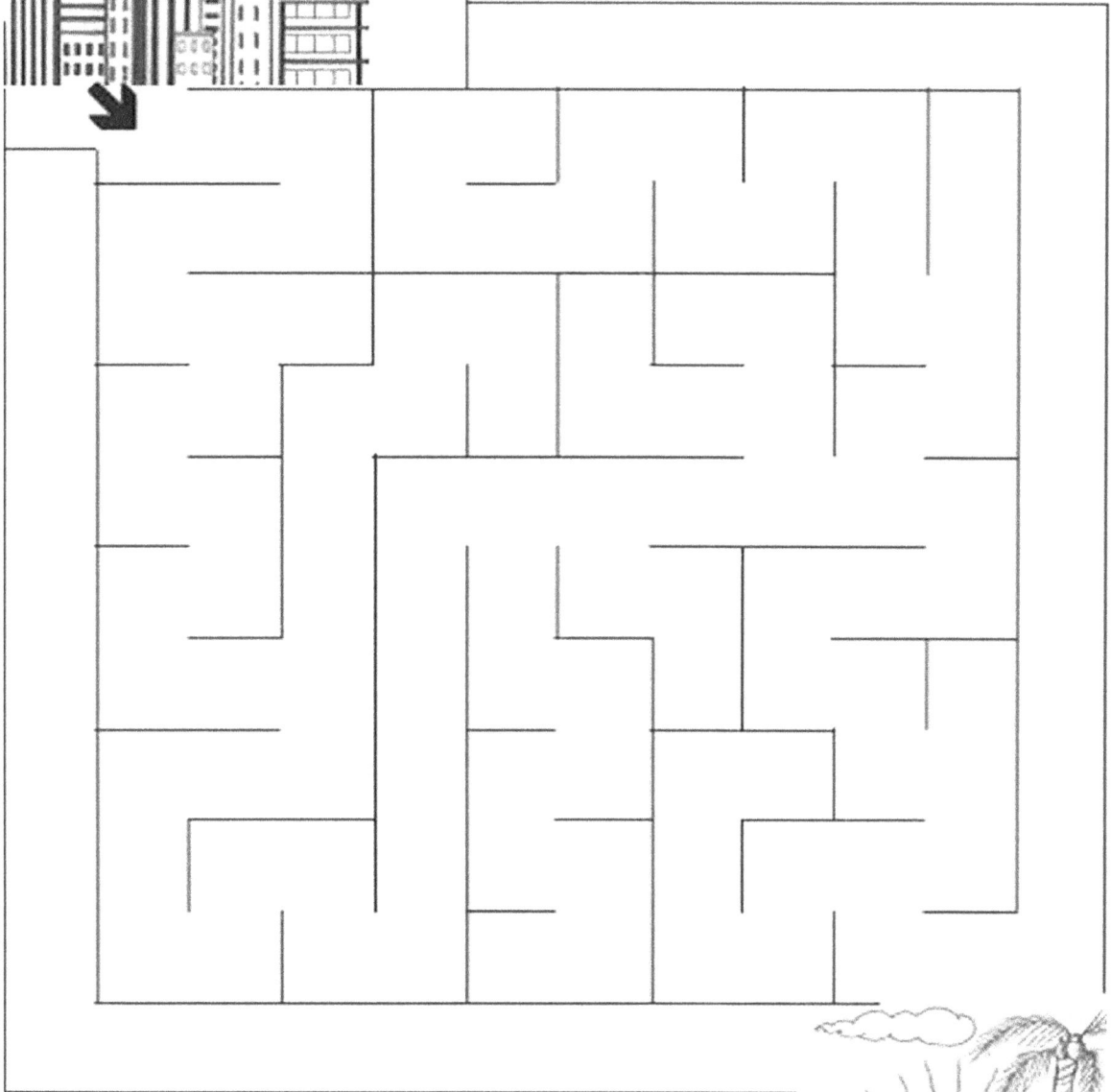

Perseverance and Problem Solving

SEQUENCE OF EVENTS

NUMBER THESE SCENES
IN THE ORDER IN WHICH THEY OCCURRED

Perseverance and Problem Solving

GLOSSARY

Perseverance and Problem-Solving

Snowbound!

perseverance — *continued effort in spite of difficulties*

problem-solving — *finding the way out of a difficulty, or finding a solution*

snowdrift — *heap of snow piled up by the wind*

expedition — *trip for a specific, or special, purpose*

stranded — *left in a helpless position*

maintenance — *keeping in a desirable or working condition*

de-iced — *prevented or removed ice-formations*

feat — *an act of achievement, usually showing courage, skills, strength, etc.*

blizzard — *storm with heavy snow, strong winds, and bitter cold*

considerably — *a great amount or extent*

temporarily — *for a limited time, or not permanent*

frantic — *wild with excitement, fear, or anxiety*

snowbound — *shut in, or closed in, by snow, or not able to get out because of snow*

back roads — *streets off the main roads*

diesel fumes — *smoke or vapor from fuel used to operate a bus engine*

permeated — *spread throughout an area*

shuttle — *plane, train, etc. that makes short trips back and forth between two places*

companions — *people who share the work, play, or interests of others*

If your plan is for one year, plant rice;
if your plan is for ten years, plant trees;
if your plan is for 100 years, educate children.

— Confucius

Confidence and Enthusiasm

VOCABULARY WORDS:

enthusiasm	visibility
occurred	confident
continent	eager
preserve	treacherous
generation	anxious
authentic	gravel
festivities	runway
port	crew
peninsula	awaited

GOING TO ANTARCTICA!

Mr. Germain's bags were packed and he was on his way to the Miami International Airport when it occurred to him that it was really happening ... he was actually going on an expedition to Antarctica! He would be flying seven hours to Santiago, the capital and largest city in Chile, South America, on a "red-eye" flight that was leaving at midnight. He could hardly wait to get started on his journey to this far-away continent.

Upon arriving at the airport, Mr. Germain checked his bags and walked quickly to the gate where other travelers were waiting for the flight to Santiago. Time seemed to move slowly, but finally he heard the announcement for the passengers to begin boarding the plane. Mr. Germain found his seat next to the window, put on his seatbelt, and settled in for the long trip. The plane took off at midnight, right on schedule.

From up in the air, Mr. Germain looked down on the city of Santiago. Upon landing, he picked up his baggage and met up with the other expedition members who had arrived from many different countries: three teachers, four students, and the expedition's team leader. After a nap at the hotel, they all met in the courtyard near the pool to discuss the purpose of Mission Antarctica: *to help preserve Antarctica, the coldest, windiest, highest, and driest continent on earth, for future generations.* Peter, the team leader, gave out special blue zippered jackets to use in the cold weather of Antarctica. It was summer there, but that meant that the temperature went up to only about five degrees!

What a time to be in Santiago ... New Year's Eve! After a delicious dinner at an authentic Indian restaurant, the team members walked downtown to where the celebrations were taking place. The night was filled with fun and fireworks. It was a wonderful way to spend time with new friends and begin a new year. After the festivities, a very tired team went back to the hotel and went to sleep, dreaming of the exciting days ahead.

The next morning, the group took a three-hour flight from Santiago to a quiet little town called Punta Arenas, which was a port used by old-time whalers. It was from this small town that they would be leaving for the ice of King George Island, in the Antarctic Peninsula. At least that was the plan. It was up to the constantly changing winds to decide whether or not their small plane would be able to take off.

The weather did not cooperate. There was just not enough wind to break up the fog that blocked the visibility to fly. After more than nine hours of waiting and waiting and *waiting*, the disappointed team headed back to the hotel to go to sleep and wonder what the next day would bring.

Morning came, and with it good weather. Incredible! The moment was finally here! They were going to Antarctica! A minivan took the group from the hotel back to the Punta Arenas airport. This time, everyone felt more confident about actually taking off because it was a bright, sunny day.

The team boarded the small plane and found their seats. With only nine seats on the aircraft, everyone was packed in like sardines in a tin can, but they were all eager to go and spirits were high. Mr. Germain stayed in the back of the plane to draw a sketch of his new team members.

It was a three-hour flight over the treacherous, icy waters of the Drake Passage, which connected the Atlantic and Pacific Oceans. The hum of the plane carried them toward the ice of Antarctica. It was cold inside the aircraft at ten degrees and

Confidence and Enthusiasm

even colder outside at minus-forty. It reminded Mr. Germain of days long ago waiting for the school bus in December in Buffalo, New York. School was not called off, even though the snowdrifts were taller than he was. Still, cold is cold, and he felt it coming through the cabin door.

The team members were a bit anxious. They all knew that if the weather changed again, they might have to turn back, but finally, after a long while, they were told that they would be able to land. Mr. Germain was filled with excitement. He had never been so far. Soon they would be there.

Mr. Germain and his teammates kept looking out of the four windows of the plane. At long last, someone saw land. They also spotted *2041*, the sixty-seven-foot yacht that they would be living and traveling on for the next ten days. The plane landed at Bellingshausen, a Russian scientific research station on King George Island. A gravel road served as a short runway with water on both sides, causing a rough landing, but the team didn't mind. They were eager to get off the plane and meet the crew of *2041*, who would be leading them in the adventures that awaited them in Antarctica.

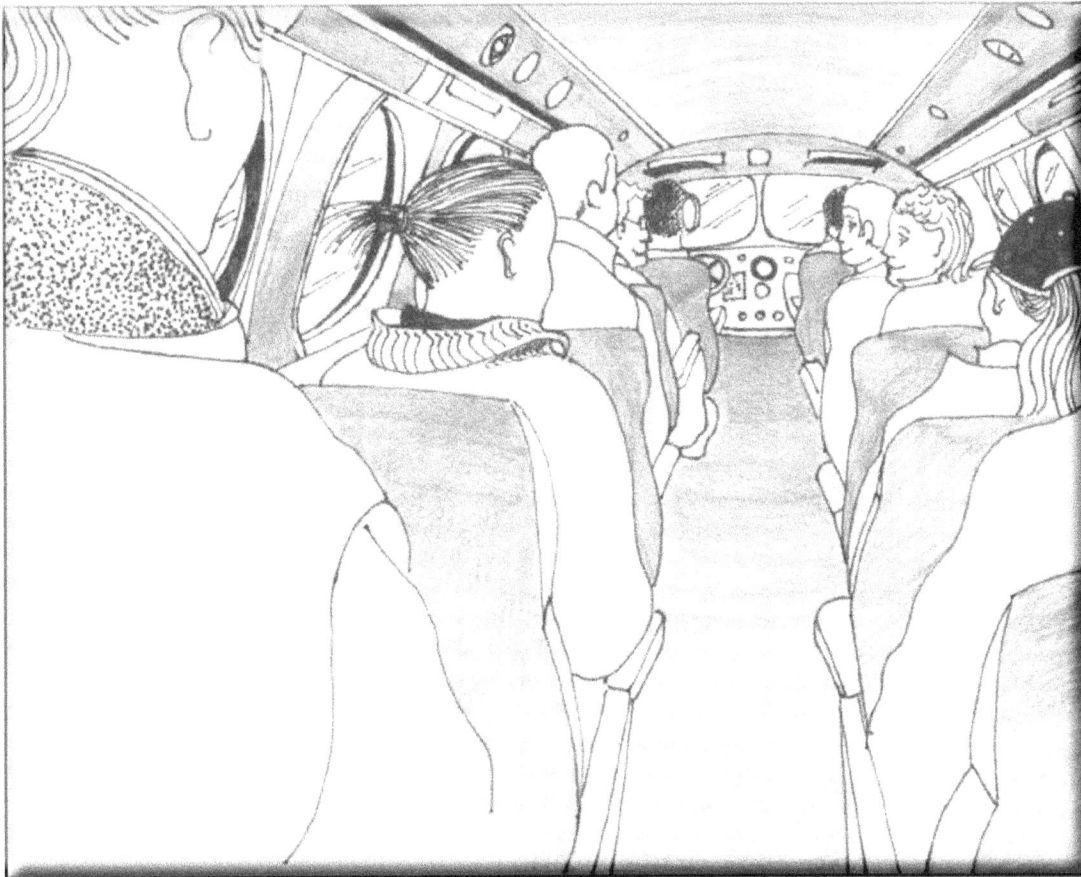

Confidence and Enthusiasm

DISCUSSION QUESTIONS:

1. Mr. Germain flew to Santiago, Chile on a midnight flight. Why do you think this would be called a "red-eye" flight?
2. What was the purpose of Mission Antarctica?
3. What special celebration took place in Santiago that also took place in the United States? Was it celebrated in the same way? How could you tell?
4. The group was anxious to leave for the Antarctic Peninsula. What did their leaving depend upon?
5. What changed the group's anxiety to confidence?
6. How did Mr. Germain connect the cold inside the aircraft with waiting for the school bus when he was a child?
7. How did the group show their enthusiasm?
8. Mr. Germain was filled with excitement because he had never been so far. What else might he have been feeling?
9. What was the *2041*?
10. What was the job of the crew of *2041*?

THOUGHT QUESTION!

Think of a time when you were anxious about something that you were going to do. How would you describe these feelings to a friend?

ACTIVITIES:

MAP STUDY
Find the following on a map: Punta Arenas, Chile; King George Island (Antarctic Peninsula); Drake Passage (locate and describe from the Encyclopedia)

VOCABULARY MATCH-UP
Match the vocabulary words with their definitions.   *(See activity page.)*

LEVEL OF CONFIDENCE:
Check your level of confidence in various situations.   *(See activity page.)*

ME COLLAGE:
Share your "Me Collage" with family members or friends.   *(See activity page.)*

Confidence and Enthusiasm

VOCABULARY MATCH-UP

MATCH THE VOCABULARY WORDS WITH THEIR DEFINITIONS

Vocabulary Words

_____	enthusiasm	_____	visibility
_____	occurred	_____	confidence
_____	continent	_____	eager
_____	preserve	_____	treacherous
_____	generation	_____	anxious
_____	authentic	_____	gravel
_____	festivities	_____	runway
_____	port	_____	crew
_____	peninsula	_____	awaited

Definitions

A. to keep from harm or maintain

B. paved or cleared strip where planes take off and land

C. full of desire or greatly looking forward to

D. strong and joyous feeling of interest

E. one of the seven large divisions of land on the earth

F. greatly worried or uneasy

G. sure, certain, or having a strong belief

H. genuine, true, or trustworthy

I. area of land almost entirely surrounded by water except for a portion connecting it to the mainland

J. took place or happened

K. celebrations or rejoicings

L. distance at which things can be seen under given conditions

M. was waiting for or was ready for

N. place where ships may dock and load or unload

O. mixture of small stones and pebbles

P. all of the people who are born at about the same time

Q. deceptive, dangerous, or not to be trusted

R. people working on a ship or aircraft

Confidence and Enthusiasm

LEVEL OF CONFIDENCE

Check your level of confidence in the following situations

	High	Medium	Low
1. When you study for a test you are having the next day	____	____	____
2. When you give a report in front of a group of people	____	____	____
3. When you walk into a room where you know only a few people	____	____	____
4. When you don't study for a test	____	____	____
5. When you feel embarrassed about a situation	____	____	____
6. When you've been told you've done a good job	____	____	____
7. When someone pays you a compliment	____	____	____
8. When you work on a group project with other peple	____	____	____
9. When you are proud of something you have accomplished	____	____	____
10. When you are playing in team sports	____	____	____
11. When you are trying out for a talent show	____	____	____
12. When you are performing in front of people	____	____	____

Describe Your Feelings:

1.When do you feel most confident?

2. When do you feel least confident? What can you do to feel more confident in this type of situation?

Confidence and Enthusiasm

"ME COLLAGE"

MR. GERMAIN MET HIS TEAM MEMBERS AND SPENT TIME GETTING TO KNOW THEM. IF YOU WERE ONE OF HIS TEAM MEMBERS, WHAT WOULD YOU TELL HIM ABOUT YOURSELF?

What interests do you have at home and at school/work? Who are the members of your family? What are your favorite hobbies, foods, books, etc.

Write a different word or phrase about yourself in each puzzle piece. Share your "Me Collage" with family members and/or friends.

Confidence and Enthusiasm

GLOSSARY
Confidence and Ethusiasm
Going to Antarctica

enthusiasm — *strong and joyous feeling of interest*

occurred — *took place or happened*

continent — *one of the seven large divisions of land on the earth*

preserve — *to keep from harm or maintain*

generation — *all of the people who are born at about the same time*

authentic — *genuine, true or trustworthy*

festivities — *celebrations or rejoicings*

port — *place where ships may dock and load or unload*

peninsula — *area of land almost entirely surrounded by water except for a portion connecting it to the mainland*

visibility — *distance at which things can be seen under given conditions*

confident — *sure, certain, or having a strong belief*

eager — *full of desire or greatly looking forward to*

treacherous — *deceptive, dangerous, unreliable, or not to be trusted*

anxious— *greatly worried or uneasy*

gravel — *mixture of small stones and pebbles*

SOUTH
ATLANTIC OCEAN

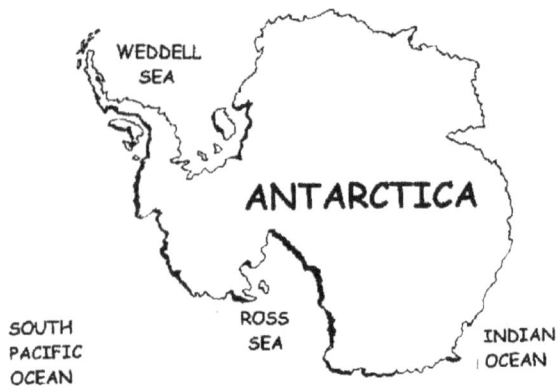

WEDDELL
SEA

ANTARCTICA

SOUTH
PACIFIC
OCEAN

ROSS
SEA

INDIAN
OCEAN

runway — *paved or cleared strip where planes take off and land*

crew — *people working on a ship or aircraft*

awaited — *was waiting for or was ready for*

Confidence and Enthusiasm

Confidence and Enthusiasm

The world is round
and the place that may
seem like the end
is only the beginning.

– Ivy Baker Priest

Determination and Tolerance

VOCABULARY WORDS:

symbolic	insecure
remarkable	barge
friction	freighter
miraculous	eventual
terrain	recycling
composed	pristine
excursion	determination
keenly	novel
endanger	tolerance
anticipation	customs

THE PLACE NEAR THE BOTTOM OF THE WORLD

Going to Antarctica was more than just a physical journey. It was a symbolic one as well. Antarctica belongs to no one; it is the only non-country on the planet. There are no religions and no ownership. There are no armies and no war. What you find instead is a sharing of scientific and environmental information. It is a remarkable example of cooperation among nations without the friction or competition that is a part of the rest of the planet. The team members were constantly busy with video, digital, and 35mm cameras. It was difficult, however, to capture the feelings that went along with the sights that were before their eyes. It was a moment-by-moment experience, ever-changing, ever-miraculous.

Since he was seated closest to the door, Mr. Germain was the first one to step off the plane, with the eight other Voyage I expedition members and the captain and co-pilot following him. He was thrilled and honored to be at the head of this adventurous party, even if it were only for a moment. At the airstrip, Chileans, Russians, and Britons all gathered together, each in his or her different role: pilot, student, teacher, journalist, sailor, engineer and so on. Mr. Germain felt as if he were in a movie; it all seemed so unreal! It was an unfamiliar terrain composed of the familiar earth, sky, and air.

He knew that this was a different kind of land; he could feel it. This was the place near the bottom of the world!

Mr. Germain was anxious to meet the crew of the yacht *2041*: Skipper Andy, First Mate Alex, Second Mate Alf, and Engineer Mike. He had an idea what Andy would look like from a picture he had seen before leaving for the expedition. Now he and the other teammates were about to meet these crew members who would be in charge of their safety and excursions while sailing in the rough waters surrounding Antarctica. He was keenly aware of their responsibilities to be continuously on the lookout for anything that would endanger the lives or well-being of the group, either aboard the *2041* or on land.

It was a moment of anticipation when Mr. Germain spotted the crew, dressed in red suits, walking forward to greet the Voyage I team members. He knew that soon he and the others would be boarding *2041*. He felt a bit nervous because he had no experience with sailing, and that made him feel somewhat insecure. He knew, however, that learning to sail would not be the only new experience. He was excited to get started on this next chapter of his journey.

The team members and crew of Voyage I were driven a short way from the plane to the Russian scientific research base called Bellingshausen (after a famous Russian polar explorer) to see the amazing sight of the Britons and Russians working together to clean up the rubbish that had been left there over the past 35 years. They had been working very hard in the cold weather for several months, taking apart huge old oil drums, obsolete vehicles, and other waste materials. These were all put onto barges and moved onto the *Anne Boye* freighter for eventual recycling. The team could see that the hard work had paid off ... the cleanup was almost finished, right on schedule with the stated goal of Mission Antarctica: to help clean up Antarctica and keep it a pristine wilderness used only for research and education. It showed what could be accomplished with determination, organization, tolerance, and cooperative effort.

Mr. Germain and his team members said their good-byes to the workers at Bellingshausen and boarded a dinghy to go to the yacht *2041*. It took the dinghy two trips in the fog to take them to the yacht with the luggage following behind. Mr. Germain couldn't believe that thirteen people from various countries, many

Determination and Tolerance

who were strangers to each other, would all be living together on this small, sixty-seven-foot yacht for the next ten days. He knew that it was going to be quite a novel experience in itself ... sharing lives and responsibilities, showing tolerance of similarities and differences, and dealing with the customs and expectations of others. As an art teacher, Mr. Germain was well aware that it painted a very interesting picture!

Determination and Tolerance

DISCUSSION QUESTIONS:

1. What is the difference between physical and symbolic journeys?
2. How does Antarctica differ from other parts of the world?
3. Why might it be difficult to capture feelings on a camera or video that go along with what you see?
4. How would you describe Mr. Germain's feeling that he was in a movie?
5. How might you compare Mr. Germain's meeting the crew of the yacht with meeting a new teacher or new classmates the first day of school?
6. Describe the responsibilities of the crew during the expedition.
7. Why did Mr. Germain feel nervous and insecure when he first spotted the crew?
8. What is Bellingshausen? What were the British and Russian cleanup crew doing there? How did the hard work pay off? What kind of effort did it take? How was determination shown at Bellingshausen?
9. How would you feel living on a small yacht with twelve strangers?
10. How might the Voyage I team members and crew show tolerance during the expedition? How might tolerance be demonstrated among friends or classmates?

THOUGHT QUESTION!

If you were offered the opportunity to go on an expedition anywhere on the planet Earth, where would you go and why? How do you think you would feel when you got there?

ACTIVITIES:

MAP STUDY
Find the following locations on a map: Chile; Russia; Great Britain; King George Island, Antarctica

VOCABULARY MATCH-UP
Match the vocabulary words with their definitions   (See activity page.)

DETERMINATION:
Use an alphabet code to discover an important message   (See activity page.)

WHAT'S THE POINT?:
Understanding tolerance   (See activity page.)

Determination and Tolerance

VOCABULARY MATCH-UP

MATCH THE VOCABULARY WORDS WITH THEIR DEFINITIONS

Vocabulary Words

_____	symbolic	_____	insecure
_____	remarkable	_____	barge
_____	friction	_____	freighter
_____	miraculous	_____	eventual
_____	terrain	_____	recycling
_____	composed	_____	pristine
_____	excursion	_____	determination
_____	keenly	_____	novel
_____	endanger	_____	tolerance
_____	anticipation	_____	customs

Definitions

A. pure and unspoiled
B. allowing other people to have opinions or follow customs that are different from one's own
C. short trip made by a group of people for a special purpose or for pleasure
D. worthy of notice or attention, or beyond the usual
E. ship for carrying goods or merchandise, rather than passengers
F. outline or surface of the land
G. boat with a flat bottom used to carry heavy objects or goods
H. expectation or a looking forward with pleasure
I. disagreement or irritation
J. coming to a decision and sticking with the belief or action
K. used as a sign for or representing something else
L. habits or generally accepted ways of doing things
M. happening as the result of events or conditions
N. sharply or in an alert manner
O. wonderful or marvelous, or beyond the usual
P. new and different from what has been known before
Q. to put in danger or at risk of harm
R. processing or treating metal, glass, etc. for reuse
S. made up or put together
T. shaky, or lacking in self-confidence

Determination and Tolerance

DETERMINATION

MR. GERMAIN IS SENDING YOU AN IMPORTANT MESSAGE USING A SPECIAL CODE.

Directions: Use the alphabet code below to discover what the message says. The first word has been filled in for you.

Alphabet Code

A	B	C	D	E	F	G	H	I	J	K	L	M
1	2	3	4	5	6	7	8	9	10	11	12	13

N	O	P	Q	R	S	T	U	V	W	X	Y	Z
14	15	16	17	18	19	20	21	22	23	24	25	26

Important Message

T h e ___ ___ ___ ___ — ___ ___ ___ ___ — ___ ___ ___ ___ — ___ ___ ___ ...
20 8 5 — 8 1 18 4 — 23 15 18 11 — 16 1 9 4 — 15 6 6

___ ___ ___ — ___ ___ ___ ___ ___ ___ ___ — ___ ___ — ___ ___ ___
20 8 5 — 3 12 5 1 14 21 16 — 2 25 — 20 8 5

___ ___ ___ ___ ___ ___ ___ — ___ ___ ___ — ___ ___ ___ ___ ___ ___ ___ — ___ ___ ___ ___
18 21 19 19 9 1 14 — 1 14 4 — 2 18 9 20 9 19 8 — 20 5 1 13

___ ___ ___ — ___ ___ ___ ___ ___ ___ — ___ ___ ___ ___ ___ ___ ___ ___ — ___ ___ ___ ___ ___
23 1 19 — 1 12 13 15 19 20 — 6 9 14 9 19 8 5 4 — 18 9 7 8 20

___ ___ — ___ ___ ___ ___ ___ ___ ___ ___ — ___ ___ ___ ___ — ___ ___ ___
15 14 — 19 3 8 5 4 21 12 5 — 23 9 20 8 — 20 8 5

___ ___ ___ ___ ___ ___ — ___ ___ ___ ___ — ___ ___ — ___ ___ ___ ___ ___ ___ ___
19 20 1 20 5 4 — 7 15 1 12 — 15 8 — 13 9 19 19 9 15 14

___ ___ ___ ___ ___ ___ ___ ___ ___ ___ — ___ ___ — ___ ___ ___ ___ — ___ ___ ___ ___ ___
1 14 20 1 18 3 20 9 3 1 — 20 15 — 8 5 12 16 — 3 12 5 1 14

___ ___ — ___ ___ ___ ___ ___ ___ ___ ___ ___ ___ — ___ ___ ___ — ___ ___ ___ ___ — ___ ___
21 16 — 1 14 20 1 18 3 20 9 3 1 — 1 14 4 — 11 5 5 16 — 9 20

___ — ___ ___ ___ ___ ___ ___ ___ ___ — ___ ___ ___ ___ ___ ___ ___ ___ ___ ___
1 — 16 18 9 19 20 9 14 5 — 23 9 12 4 5 18 14 5 19 19

___ ___ ___ ___ — ___ ___ ___ ___ — ___ ___ ___ — ___ ___ ___ ___ ___ ___ ___ ___
21 19 5 4 — 15 14 12 25 — 6 15 18 — 18 5 19 5 1 18 3 8

___ ___ ___ — ___ ___ ___ ___ ___ ___ ___ ___ ___ — ___ ___ — ___ ___ ___ ___ ___ ___
1 14 4 — 5 4 21 3 1 20 9 15 14 — 9 20 — 19 8 15 23 5 4

___ ___ ___ ___ — ___ ___ ___ ___ ___ — ___ ___
23 8 1 20 — 3 15 21 12 4 — 2 5

___ ___ ___ ___ ___ ___ ___ ___ ___ ___ ___ ___ — ___ ___ ___ ___
1 3 3 15 13 16 12 9 19 8 5 4 — 23 9 20 8

___ ___ ___ ___ ___ ___ ___ ___ ___ ___ ___ ___ ___ — ___ ___ ___ — ___ ___ ___ ___ ___ ___ .
4 5 20 5 18 13 9 14 1 20 9 15 14 — 1 14 4 — 5 6 6 15 18 20

Determination and Tolerance

WHAT'S THE POINT?

TOLERANCE BEGINS WITH UNDERSTANDING. WHAT'S THE POINT OF GETTING TO KNOW OTHER PEOPLE AND HAVING THEM GET TO KNOW YOU? WHEN PEOPLE LEARN TO UNDERSTAND THEIR SIMILARITIES AND TO APPRECIATE THEIR DIFFERENCES, THEY GET ALONG BETTER.

Directions: IN EACH OF THE GLACIER'S PEAKS, WRITE ABOUT YOURSELF:

1. Write your first and last name; from what country did your last name originate?
2. In what country were you born? Your parents? Your grandparents?
3. What are some of the foods that are special to your family or country?
4. What music is special to your family's country or countries of origin?
5. What holidays are special to your family's country or countries of origin?
6. What language or languages do you speak at home? Within the community?

When you have completed this exercise, share your answers with friends or family members. Note some of the similarities and differences.

What have you learned by doing this exercise and sharing it with others?

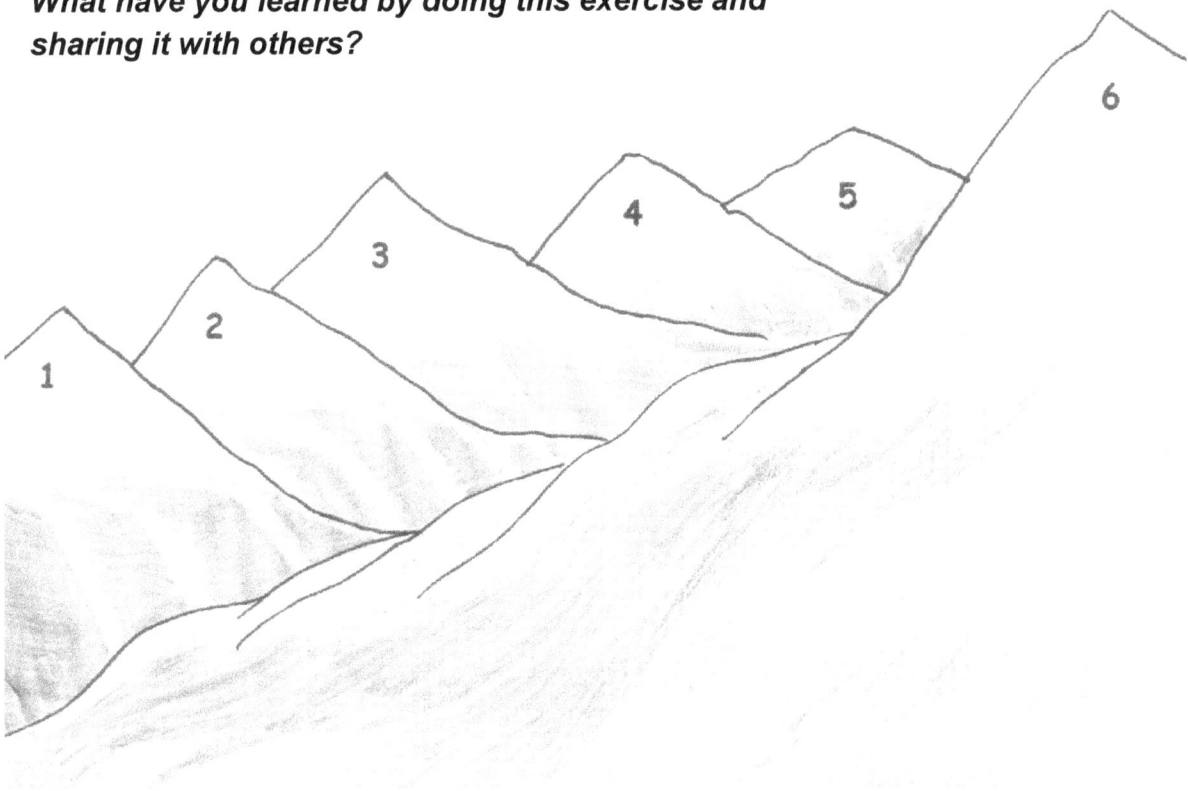

Determination and Tolerance

GLOSSARY

Determination and Tolerance
The Place Near the Bottom of the World

symbolic — *used as a sign for or representing something else*

remarkable — *worthy of notice or attention, or beyond the usual*

friction — *disagreement or irritation*

miraculous — *wonderful or marvelous, or beyond the usual*

terrain — *outline or surface of the land*

composed — *made up or put together*

excursion — *short trip made by a group of people for a special purpose or for pleasure*

keenly — *sharply or in an alert manner*

endanger — *to put in danger or at risk of harm*

anticipation — *expectation or a looking forward with pleasure*

insecure — *shaky, or lacking self-confidence*

barge — *boat with a flat bottom used to carry heavy objects or goods*

freighter — *ship for carrying goods or merchandise, rather than passengers*

eventual — *happening as the result of events or conditions*

recycling — *processing or treating metal, glass, etc. for reuse*

pristine — *pure and unspoiled*

determination — *coming to a decision and sticking with the belief or action*

novel — *new and different from what has been known before*

tolerance — *allowing other people to have opinions or follow customs that are different from one's own*

customs — *habits or generally accepted ways of doing things*

Determination and Tolerance

Determination and Tolerance

*It is not genius, not glory, nor love
that reflects the greatness of the
human soul; it is kindness.*

— Henri-Dominique Lacordaire

Respect and Sharing

Respect and Sharing

VOCABULARY WORDS:

sharing	privacy
respect	scarce
refitted	galley
expedition	quarters
rigorous	cramped
impression	tours
surroundings	adjusting
pitched	expectant
secured	

SHARING SPACE

The yacht *2041* had been built for the World Challenger Cup Races and then refitted to meet the needs of the rigorous Mission Antarctica expeditions. Mr. Germain's first impression as he stepped onto the yacht was how small it was. He wondered how the team members and crew were all going to live together for ten days. He looked around the yacht, taking in the layout of his surroundings.

Tables, counters, cabinets, etc. below deck had railings around them so that nothing would fall off when the yacht rolled and pitched in the waves. Things were folding and stackable and were made of plastic. Everything was put away in its own space. There were six areas for sleeping, two of which were taken by the crew. All of the beds were bunk beds except for one single bed that looked like it was in a small cave. Mr. Germain chose that bed. He had to crawl into the space in order to lie down on the bed, taking care not to bump his head!

Sharing of space was a necessity. Each person unpacked and put his or her belongings into a plastic box that slid into the wall. The boxes had to be secured because everything swayed with the rocking of the yacht. Mr. Germain noticed the wires that ran the length of the deck. On it were hooks for the team members and

Respect and Sharing

crew to latch on to while they were on deck. One thing that wasn't needed was for someone to get injured or fall overboard!

It didn't take long for Mr. Germain to understand how little privacy there was on the yacht. It was quite snug indeed! There was only one bathroom for everyone to share. Since there was only one shower, team members and crew sometimes couldn't shower for days at a time. They used up a lot of wet wipes in place of showers. Mr. Germain thought about how much he had taken for granted the private bathroom he had at home.

The galley was a small area that included an oval-shaped booth where they all ate together. Under each cushion was storage space for food. This included dry goods such as cereal, potatoes, cake mixes and candy bars, as well as other products. Team members took turns cooking meals, which included breakfast, lunch, and dinner shifts. Mr. Germain, who loved to eat, was glad that he had learned how to cook and was hoping that the others had learned, as well!

Being on the *2041* was a new experience for all the Voyage I team members. The small quarters, shared space, and cramped living environment were no match for the enthusiasm of everyone on board. Following the safety talks and tours of the yacht, they were all up to the challenges of adjusting. Each person was excited, anxious, hopeful, and expectant ... *and raring to go!*

Respect and Sharing

DISCUSSION QUESTIONS:

1. What were Mr. Germain's concerns when he stepped onto the yacht *2041*?
2. What do you think it means to "take in the layout of your surroundings?"
3. Why did everything below deck have railings around it?
4. Why do you suppose Mr. Germain liked his "bed in a cave" better than the bunk beds?
5. How would sharing space on the yacht be similar to sharing space in school, at home, or during summer camp?
6. What was needed up on deck in order not to fall overboard?
7. What do you think is meant by the statement about the yacht: "It was quite snug, indeed?"
8. Why was Mr. Germain glad that he had learned how to cook before going on the expedition? Why did he hope that others had learned? Is there anything that you have learned to cook? Why would it be important for you to learn how to cook?
9. What was meant by the following statement: "The small quarters, shared space and cramped living environment was no match for the enthusiasm of everyone on board?"

THOUGHT QUESTION!

Mr. Germain thought about how much he might have taken for granted, such as the private bathroom he had at home. What are some of the things you take for granted?

ACTIVITIES:

VOCABULARY MATCH-UP
Match the vocabulary words with their definitions.   *(See activity page.)*

INSIDE THE 2041:
Label the areas in the *2041*.   *(See activity page.)*

TOUR GUIDE:
Describe the layout and points of interest at your school.   (See activity page.)

Respect and Sharing

VOCABULARY MATCH-UP

MATCH THE VOCABULARY WORDS WITH THEIR DEFINITIONS

Vocabulary Words

_____ sharing	_____ privacy
_____ respect	_____ scarce
_____ refitted	_____ galley
_____ rigorous	_____ quarters
_____ impression	_____ cramped
_____ surroundings	_____ tours
_____ pitched	_____ adjusting
_____ secured	_____ expectant

Definitions

A. kitchen of a ship or airplane

B. trip for a special purpose

C. using with someone, or dividing into parts

D. waiting or being ready for a planned or likely event or happening

E. restricted or limited, or lacking enough space

F. firmly tied, fixed, fastened, or closed

G. effect or impact on the mind or feelings

H. physical separateness from other people

I. made ready, repaired, or equipped for use again

J. going around from place to place to see or inspect

K. manner that shows courtesy, consideration, or high opinion

L. becoming familiar with a new place or thing, adapting, or changing so as to fit new conditions or uses

M. uncomfortably severe or harsh

N. environment (people or things around a person)

O. not available in large amounts, or hard to get

P. place to live or living area

Q. dipped the bow and stern alternately, as a ship in rough waters

Respect and Sharing

INSIDE THE 2041

LABEL THE PARTS OF THE 2041 BY USING THE WORD LIST BELOW *(ONE OF THE LABELS IS USED TWICE).*

a. cabins and berths
b. fo'c's'le
c. foulies closet
d. galley

e. head
f. navigation station
g. saloon
h. storage

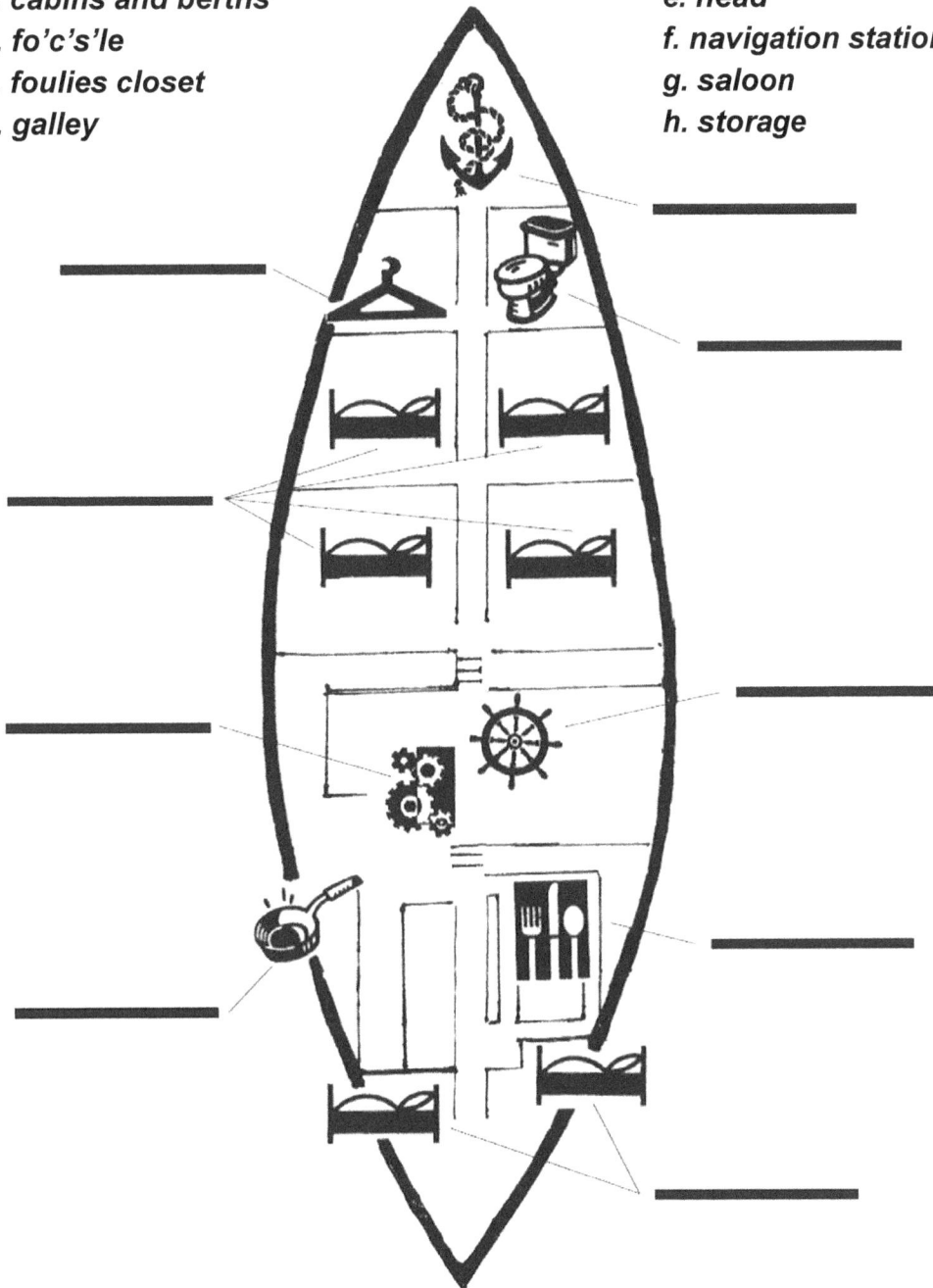

TOUR GUIDE

1. DRAW A DIAGRAM OF YOUR SCHOOL AS A GUIDE FOR NEW STUDENTS AND THEIR PARENTS.

2. ACTING AS A TOUR GUIDE AT YOUR SCHOOL, WHAT POINTS OF INTEREST WOULD YOU DESCRIBE?

Respect and Sharing

GLOSSARY
Respect and Sharing
Sharing Space

sharing — *using with someone, or dividing into parts*

respect — *manner that shows courtesy, consideration, or high opinion*

refitted — *made ready, repaired, or equipped for use again*

rigorous — *uncomfortably severe or harsh*

expedition — *trip for a special purpose*

impression — *effect or impact on the mind or feelings*

surrounding — *environment (people or things around a person)*

pitched — *dipped the bow and stern alternately, as a ship in rough waters*

secured — *firmly tied, fixed, fastened or closed*

privacy — *physical separateness from other people*

scarce — *not available in large amounts, or hard to get*

galley — *kitchen of a ship or airplane*

quarters — *place to live or living area*

cramped — *restricted or limited, or lacking enough space*

tours — *going around from place to place to see or inspect*

adjusting — *becoming familiar with a new place or thing, adapting, or changing so as to it new conditions or uses*

expectant — *waiting or being ready for a planned or likely event or happening*

INSIDE THE 2041

cabin and berths — *area with bunks (beds built like large shelves)*

fo'c's'le — *(sailor's term for forecastle) - shelter or area for equipment on the yacht*

foulies closet — *space for hanging the foulies when not being worn*

galley — *kitchen*

head — *bathroom*

navigation station — *yacht control area with radar, computers, and radar screens that check for water depth, wind speed, icebergs, etc.*

saloon — *eating or dining area*

storage — *where supplies are kept for future use*

*We're all assigned a piece of the garden,
a corner that is ours to transform.*

—Marianne Williamson

Consideration and Patience

patience
cumbersome
gear
foul-weather
outerwear
feat
suspenders
vest
soles

protection
balm
bulky
rigors
long-john
considerate
former
luxury

FOULIES

The reason there was only one bathroom for everyone's use on the yacht *2041* was that the second bathroom was used to hang up all of the foulies, which were cumbersome gear that each person had to wear above deck and on land. It was only below deck that they did not have to be worn. Foulies, which stands for foul-weather gear, were well-designed for keeping out the wet and cold. These were the hooded red outerwear that Mr. Germain saw the crew wearing when he met them at the airstrip.

The first day on the yacht there was a lesson on how to put on foulies that included when to wear them, how to get them on, and how to put them away. Putting on foulies was no easy feat! Each person was assigned a number for his or her foulies and life vest. Mr. Germain was given number 8. He listened carefully to the directions that were given to the group. First were the pants that he stepped into just as a fireman does, complete with suspenders. After that came the jacket and hood, followed by a life vest. Woolen socks were worn on his feet under his boat boots that had special soles so as not make marks on the deck. Thick gloves, a warm scarf, and a wool cap which covered his ears were added for further protection from the cold. Goggles were worn on windy days. Otherwise, sunglasses were needed along with the necessary lip balm and sunblock. Mr. Germain walked about the deck in his new foulies. He felt like an astronaut on the moon! The foulies were not only bulky but made swooshy noises as he moved around!

Every time Mr. Germain, his teammates, and the crew left their warmer cozy space beneath the deck, they had to go through the rigors of putting on all of their cold-weather gear. Underneath the foulies they wore silk long-john tops and bottoms covered by light clothing. They also wore cotton socks under their wool socks for added comfort and warmth. You can just imagine how little dressing space there was and how considerate each person had to be of others in the group. If someone said, "Come up on deck and look at the whales, or seals, or birds!" they all had to first put on their foulies before going up on deck to see what was happening.

Mr. Germain joined the others in taking off all of their foul-weather gear and hanging them up in the former bathroom. Since that was the only space left on the yacht to keep the foulies, he would just have to accept that the luxury of a second bathroom on the *2041* would have to remain a dream.

Consideration and Patience

DISCUSSION QUESTIONS:

1. How would it be to have a small apartment with 13 people and only one bathroom? How would it affect the people who had to go to school or work? Why would being considerate be important?
2. Why was it necessary for Mr. Germain to listen to directions during the lesson on foulies? When might it be important for you to listen to directions at school? At home?
3. Why did Mr. Germain feel like an astronaut on the moon when he walked about the deck in his new foulies? Since Mr. Germain had never been to the moon, how was he able to compare the two situations? Never having worn foulies, could you still imagine how it would feel?
4. In what professions are bulky clothes or equipment worn? What have you ever worn that felt bulky?
5. Why was it a hardship putting on the cold-weather gear? Why couldn't the team members and crew put on their foulies up on the deck where there was more room? In what way did they have to be considerate of each other?
6. Where did the team members and crew hang their foulies? What did they have to give up in order to have the space to hang them?

THOUGHT QUESTION!

Think of all the things you have needed or wanted. Make two lists: What would you put in the "need" list? What would you put in the "want" list? Go through the "need" list. What could be moved over to the "want" list? What did you realize by doing this exercise? Are most things needs or luxuries?

ACTIVITIES:

VOCABULARY MATCH-UP
Match the vocabulary words with their definitions.   *(See activity page.)*

GET YOUR FOULIES ON!:
Label the items that Mr. Germain is wearing.   *(See activity page.)*

CONSIDERATION AND PATIENCE:
Write your perspective.   *(See activity page.)*

Consideration and Patience

VOCABULARY MATCH-UP

MATCH THE VOCABULARY WORDS WITH THEIR DEFINITIONS

Vocabulary Words

_____	patience	_____	protection
_____	cumbersome	_____	balm
_____	gear	_____	bulky
_____	foul-weather	_____	rigors
_____	outerwear	_____	long-john
_____	feat	_____	considerate
_____	suspenders	_____	former
_____	vest	_____	luxury
_____	soles		

Definitions

A. heavy or troublesome (bulky)

B. sleeveless jacket, usually worn over a shirt

C. ointment that heals or soothes

D. thoughtful of others or kind

E. stormy or severe conditions

F. massive, big, or broad

G. action that shows great courage, skill, or strength

H. bottoms of shoes, boots, or slippers

I. being able to delay or wait for something without complaint

J. garment worn under clothing to keep a person warm in cold weather

K. straps worn over the shoulders to hold up trousers (pants)

L. clothing that is worn over other clothing

M. something that is not necessary for life, but can make it more enjoyable or comfortable

N. hardships

O. keeping safe, guarding or defending from danger or injury

P. equipment or clothing

Q. having been in the past

Consideration and Patience

GET YOUR FOULIES ON

LABEL THE ITEMS THAT MR. GERMAIN IS WEARING BY USING THE LIST ON THE LEFT SIDE OF THE PAGE.

A. WOOLEN SOCKS
   (underneath)

B. GOGGLES

C. FOULIES NUMBER

D. LIP BALM
   (underneath)

E. COTTON SOCKS
   (underneath)

F. LIFE VEST

G. MITTENS

H. WOOLEN CAP

I. SUSPENDERS
   (underneath)

J. PANTS

K. SCARF

L. LONG JOHNS
   (underneath)

M. BOAT BOOTS

N. JACKET

O. HARNESS LINE

(underneath)

(underneath)

(underneath)

#8

(underneath)

(underneath)

(underneath)

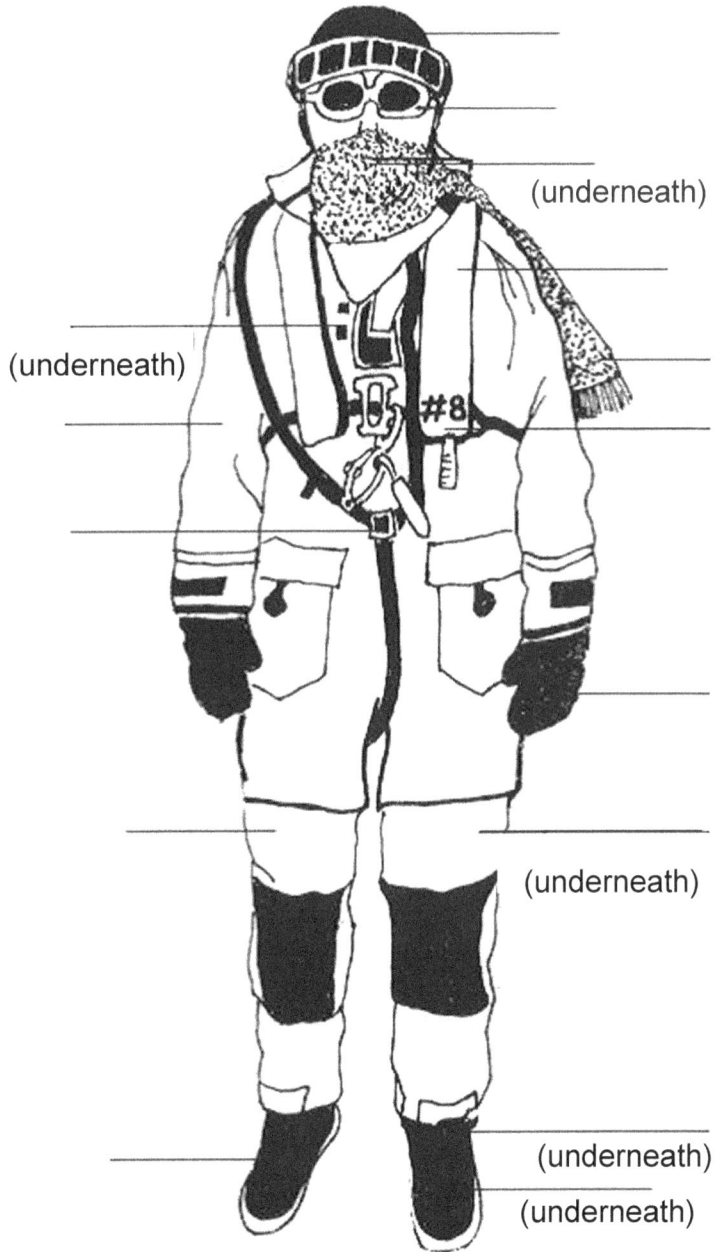

Consideration and Patience

CONSIDERATION AND PATIENCE

1. WRITE ABOUT A TIME YOU WERE CONSIDERATE OF ANOTHER PERSON'S FEELINGS, OR ANOTHER PERSON WAS CONSIDERATE OF YOUR FEELINGS.

2. WRITE A SLOGAN ABOUT BEING CONSIDERATE OF OTHERS. SHARE YOUR SLOGAN WITH OTHERS AT HOME OR AT SCHOOL.

3. TELL ABOUT A TIME YOU SHOWED PATIENCE IN A DIFFICULT SITUATION.

Consideration and Patience

GLOSSARY

Consideration and Patience
Foulies

patience — *being able to delay or wait for something without complaint*

cumbersome — *heavy or troublesome (bulky)*

gear — *equipment or clothing*

foul-weather — *stormy or severe conditions*

outerwear — *clothing that is worn over other clothing*

feat — *action that shows great courage, skill, or strength*

suspenders — *straps worn over the shoulders to hold up trousers (pants)*

vest — *sleeveless jacket, usually worn over a shirt*

soles — *bottoms of shoes, boots, or slippers*

protection — *keeping safe, guarding or defending from danger or injury*

balm — *ointment that heals or soothes*

bulky — *massive, big, or broad*

rigors — *hardships*

long-john — *garment worn under clothing to keep a person warm in cold weather*

considerate — *thoughtful of others or kind*

former — *having been in the past*

luxury — *something that is not necessary for life, but can make it more enjoyable*

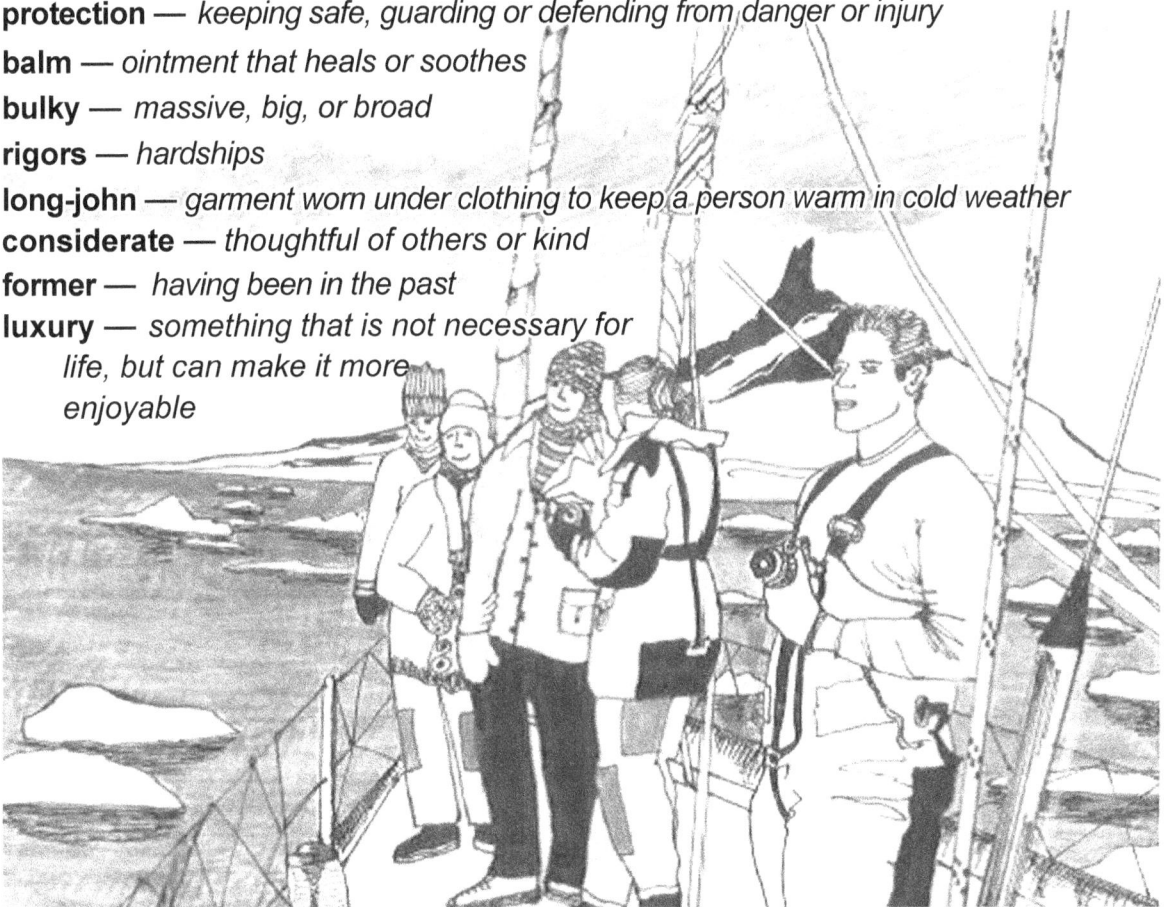

Character is what you do
when no one is looking.

—unknown

Common Sense
and Cooperation

VOCABULARY WORDS:

common sense	aspect
cooperation	emphasized
glacier	procedures
awesome	discarding
iceberg	biodegradable
logical	hefty
factual	litter
grasp	unstable
concepts	radar
envied	forged
glimpse	displayed

LESSONS LEARNED

It was a very full day with sailing lessons in the morning and galley lessons, as well. The crew took the Voyage I team on their first expedition out to a glacier. Mr. Germain couldn't believe the awesome sights! He assisted with the ropes the best he could, but he knew nothing about the world of sailing. He kept his eyes and ears open because he needed to learn enough to do his share of the work. Being an art teacher, the artistic, creative right side of his brain seemed to take over the more logical, factual left side! He was the target of good-natured jokes as he tried to grasp the concepts of Yankee sails, main sails, and staysails, as well as winching, knots, and wind direction. It was like learning a whole new language. He envied the crew for their lives as wandering sailors. All of them had been around the world, some more than once. He knew he was going to get a glimpse of the life of a sailor during his days on the yacht *2041*. Mr. Germain figured that he traveled the world in his own way, making art.

Skipper Andy, a big bear of a man from Great Britain, took over for the lesson on safety, which was the most important aspect of the expedition. He emphasized that each person was responsible, not only for the safety of himself or herself, but for the safety of each other. It was a time to be aware of yourself and the rest of the team. It was important to stay warm, yet, at the same time, not get too hot.

It was stressed that they were on an expedition and wouldn't know weather-wise what they were dealing with ... it depended on what the changeable weather threw at them at any given time. It was expected that, for the most part, they would be in protected waters; however, they would also be crossing more forceful seas which involved looking out for yourself and others.

There was the physical safety of being in cramped quarters, as well as hooking yourself to the wires that ran the length of the deck. Moving around was not easy, whether below deck or on deck, since the yacht was in constant motion.

There were also procedures for discarding garbage on the yacht *2041*. Anything that was biodegradable, such as food scraps, was thrown overboard. Cardboard, like cereal boxes, first had to be torn into very small pieces. Anything that was not biodegradable was kept in hefty bags for drop off at one of the scientific bases.

Before leaving for shore, Andy discussed how the team members should behave, what not to do, and how to be careful when around the variety of animals they would see. He felt it was especially refreshing when the students asked if they could pick up any litter, and take it away with them. Andy felt that already they were making a difference and hoped that the environmental message would reach more people when they returned home from their Antarctic journey.

It was explained to the Voyage I team that only one-sixth to one-third of an iceberg could be seen above water. Since the largest portion of an iceberg was underwater, it could easily be a threat to the yacht and the safety of all persons on board. The team also learned that icebergs melted over time, often causing them to become unstable and flip. Throughout

Common Sense and Cooperation

their journey, all team members had to take turns keeping watch on a radar screen for possible icebergs that might be in the way of the yacht as it forged through the water. It was also important at all times to stay aware of the changeable winds. If they died down, the person on watch had to wake Skipper Andy so that he could take charge of the situation.

Being a forceful, in-command captain of the *2041*, Skipper Andy displayed his no-nonsense approach early in the journey. The teachers were told that it was necessary to turn off the lights when they weren't being used. When they forgot, Skipper Andy reminded them. When they continued forgetting, he removed the bulb. Mr. Germain found himself reading by flashlight. The teachers were quite embarrassed about their punishment, especially with the students on board!

Common Sense and Cooperation

DISCUSSION QUESTIONS:

1. Where did the crew take the Voyage I team on their first expedition?
2. Did Mr. Germain know anything about sailing? What did he do about it?
3. Why did Mr. Germain think he needed to use the "logical, factual left side" of his brain? When do you use this side of your brain?
4. Mr. Germain tried to "grasp the concepts" of a whole new sailing language. How does this compare to students who come to your country and have to learn a new language in school? How do you think they feel?
5. What is meant by a "good-natured joke?" Could feelings be hurt?
6. What do you think Mr. Germain meant when he figured he "traveled the world in his own way, making art?"
7. How would you describe a "big bear of a man?" Might he have a beard?
8. Why was safety the most important aspect of the expedition? Why is safety the most important aspect of school?
9. Why were the crew and team members responsible for not only themselves, but for each other, as well? In what way is that similar to situations with students at school?
10. What were the procedures for discarding garbage on the yacht *2041*? Why was this important? How do you help to take care of your environment?
11. Why did team members have to take turns watching for icebergs? Why might they have to be aware of the changing winds?
12. The teachers were not acting in a responsible manner when they continuously forgot to turn off the lights. How were they "punished" by Skipper Andy? Why were they embarrassed? Have you ever felt embarrassed by your actions?

THOUGHT QUESTION!

What are some situations that might involve cooperation: at home, at school, at play?

ACTIVITIES:

VOCABULARY MATCH-UP:
Match the vocabulary words with their definitions.   *(See activity page.)*

COMMON SENSE AND COOPERATION:
Thought question   *(See activity page.)*

ANIMAL ENVY:
Thought questions that promote self-understanding   *(See activity page.)*

WORD SEARCH:
Circle the vocabulary words.   *(See activity page.)*

SAILING ... A NEW LANGUAGE:
Learning the parts of the yacht   *(See activity page.)*

Common Sense and Cooperation

VOCABULARY MATCH-UP

MATCH THE VOCABULARY WORDS WITH THEIR DEFINITIONS

Vocabulary Words

_____ common sense	_____ concepts	_____ hefty
_____ cooperation	_____ envied	_____ litter
_____ glacier	_____ glimpse	_____ unstable
_____ awesome	_____ aspect	_____ radar
_____ iceberg	_____ emphasized	_____ forged
_____ logical	_____ procedures	_____ displayed
_____ factual	_____ discarding	
_____ grasp	_____ biodegradable	

Definitions

A. paper, scraps, etc., scattered carelessly around

B. placed special value or importance on, or stressed

C. overwhelming feeling of wonder or admiration

D. able to decay or rot by natural means, especially by bacteria or fungi

E. based on what is true or real

F. judgment based on experience, or a practical way of looking at things

G. element or part

H. having feelings of jealousy

I. throwing something away, or getting rid of something that is unwanted

J. huge, moving mass of ice formed by the pressure of many snowfalls

K. device or machine that sends out radio waves in a beam that when reflected back from distant object, shows position, distance, and direction of movement

L. working together toward the same end or goal, or joint effort

M. heavy, or big and powerful

N. steadily moved forward, but with difficulty

O. short or quick look

P. mass of floating ice, often of great size, separated from the base of a glacier and carried out to sea

Q. likely to change, shaky, or shifting

R. mental images or ideas

S. full of good sense (sensible), or reasonable

T. ways or manner of getting something done

U. showed or made known

V. to hold firmly in the mind, or to understand

Common Sense and Cooperation

COMMON SENSE AND COOPERATION

COMMON SENSE TELLS US THAT GROUP MEMBERS WHO COOPERATE WITH EACH OTHER ACCOMPLISH WHAT THEY SET OUT TO DO.

GIVE AN EXAMPLE OF HOW YOU WORKED TOGETHER ON A PROJECT WITH TWO OR MORE CLASSMATES:

WHAT WAS THE PROJECT?

WHAT WAS YOUR ROLE AS A GROUP MEMBER?

WAS IT A COOPERATIVE EFFORT?

HOW DID THE PROJECT TURN OUT?

WHAT DID YOU LEARN ABOUT WORKING IN GROUPS?

Common Sense and Cooperation

ANIMAL ENVY

1. SKIPPER ANDY WAS DESCRIBED AS A "BIG BEAR OF A MAN."
IF YOU DESCRIBED YOURSELF IN TERMS OF AN ANIMAL, WHAT
ANIMAL WOULD YOU BE AND WHY?

2. WRITE ABOUT A TIME YOU ENVIED SOMEONE ELSE.
WHAT DID YOU LEARN FROM THE EXPERIENCE?

Common Sense and Cooperation

WORD SEARCH

CIRCLE THE VOCABULARY WORDS IN THE PUZZLE BELOW. THEY MAY BE FOUND GOING ACROSS, DOWN, OR DIAGONALLY.

O	U	T	R	A	D	I	S	C	A	R	D	I	N	G	B	A
L	C	F	F	C	O	O	P	E	R	A	T	I	O	N	U	L
F	O	A	T	G	N	P	B	T	W	L	G	R	A	S	P	N
B	M	C	P	R	O	C	E	D	U	R	E	S	M	T	J	C
I	M	T	D	F	W	P	E	B	K	L	O	G	I	C	A	L
O	O	U	P	U	Q	I	R	T	C	F	U	L	K	M	R	J
D	N	A	B	U	V	K	G	O	S	W	T	A	Z	B	D	G
E	S	L	I	N	D	N	L	P	C	O	N	C	E	P	T	S
G	E	C	E	S	I	M	I	O	A	K	M	I	Q	H	I	K
R	N	L	I	T	S	G	M	U	N	A	H	E	L	E	I	M
A	S	I	C	A	P	E	P	R	A	D	A	R	A	F	T	Z
D	E	T	E	B	L	J	S	A	F	I	P	E	L	T	L	E
A	Z	T	B	L	A	W	E	S	O	M	E	G	R	Y	S	F
B	M	E	E	E	Y	R	M	K	R	G	L	I	M	R	S	A
L	W	R	R	O	E	E	L	O	G	I	M	A	U	K	E	C
E	A	D	G	F	D	S	O	R	E	L	P	O	R	C	E	T
E	M	P	H	A	S	I	Z	E	D	M	C	P	G	L	A	U

Vocabulary Words

common sense	concepts	hefty
cooperation	envied	litter
glacier	glimpse	unstable
awesome	aspect	radar
iceberg	emphasized	forged
logical	procedures	displayed
factual	discarding	
grasp	biodegradable	

Common Sense and Cooperation

SAILING ... A NEW LANGUAGE

Label the parts of the yacht by using the list below:

Yankee sail — the front sail

Main sail — the big, main sail that goes up the mast

Staysail — the sail between the Main and Yankee sails

Bow — the front, pointed bit

Stern — the back of a yacht

Mast — the bit stick (pole) stuck in the middle of the yacht

Boom — the beam that goes across that is attached to the mast

Winching — using a crank for hoisting (lifting) or hauling (pulling)

Knots — units of speed used by ships and planes, equal to a rate of one nautical mile per hour

Wind direction — the direction from which the wind is blowing

Common Sense and Cooperation

GLOSSARY
Common Sense and Cooperation
Lessons Learned

common sense — *judgment based on experience, or a practical way of looking at things*

cooperation — *working together toward the same end or goal, or joint effort*

glacier — *a huge, moving mass of ice formed by the pressure of many snowfalls*

awesome — *filled with wonder or admiration*

iceberg — *mass of floating ice, often of great size, separated from the base of a glacier and carried out to sea*

logical — *full of good sense (sensible), or reasonable*

factual — *based on what is true or real*

grasp — *to hold firmly in the mind, or to understand*

concepts — *mental images or ideas*

envied — *having feelings of jealousy*

glimpse — *short or quick look*

aspect — *element or part*

emphasized — *stressed, or placed special value or importance on*

procedures — *ways or manner of getting something done*

discarding — *throwing something away, or getting rid of something that is unwanted*

biodegradable — *able to decay or rot by natural means, especially by bacteria or fungi*

hefty — *heavy, or big and powerful*

litter — *paper, scrap, etc., scattered carelessly around*

unstable — *likely to change, shaky, or shifting*

radar — *device or machine that sends out radio waves in a beam that when reflected back from a distant object, shows position, distance, and direction of movement*

forged — *steadily moved forward, but with difficulty*

displayed — *showed, or made known*

Common Sense and Cooperation

Common Sense and Cooperation

*... Know that every deed counts,
every word has power. Above all,
build your life as if it's a work of art.*

—Abraham Joshua Heschel

Commitment and Organization

VOCABULARY WORDS:

organization	military
commitment	vehicles
debris	various
embedded	abandoned
waste	metallic
accomplished	torch barge
immense	Danish
dismantled	rubbish
southerly	

BELLINGSHAUSEN AND THE ANNE BOYE

Following the sailing lessons in the morning, the Voyage I group stopped back at Bellingshausen later in the afternoon to help a bit with the cleanup. Seeing the penguins nearby returning to the nearly-cleaned-up beach made everyone want to do his or her part. The beach there had come such a long way, and the men had worked so very hard. Still, it was sad to see the debris so embedded into the soil. There were pieces of rubber, bits of wood and metal, plastic, glass, oil, and other waste materials.

The Voyage I team talked to the cleanup crew about the work they had undertaken and the stages it took to get the job accomplished. The larger equipment had to be dismantled, and the waste material had to be separated into biodegradable and non-biodegradable piles. Mr. Germain and his team members went inside the *Anne Boye,* an immense freighter with a Danish crew. The *Anne Boye* had been receiving the rubbish of the Bellingshausen cleanup — everything from bulldozers, typewriters, military vehicles, empty paint cans, oil drums, various huge scraps of metal, wood and styrofoam, to other abandoned materials. The captain of the *Anne Boye* let them have a look at the hold, where the rubbish was stored before being taken to be recycled. About three-fourths full, with approximately 800 tons of scrap, it was a metallic dump that smelled of oil and rust.

The day before, the team members and crew had seen an old boat that was being cut in two by Russian volunteers using a gas torch. They were amazed that just one day later, the remains were already sitting on top of the scrap pile on the *Anne Boye.* During the day, two more bargefuls of mainly barrels and heavy metal pieces were loaded onto the ship. It was just another day for the hard-working cleanup team at Bellingshausen.

It had been a cold and rainy day, and after having been out for over three hours, Mr. Germain was glad to go inside where he could get dry and warm. The crew was preparing to travel to another island that was more southerly in the King George Peninsula. No one knew which island they would visit. It all depended on the weather and wind direction. Skipper Andy would decide as they moved along, always aware of the safety of the team and crew.

Commitment and Organization

DISCUSSION QUESTIONS:

1. Why do you think that seeing the penguins returning to the nearly-cleaned-up beach made the team members want to do their part in helping the cleanup efforts?
2. Why was it sad to see the deeply embedded debris in the soil?
3. What was the goal of the freighter, *Anne Boye*?
4. How did a gas torch help to cut apart an old boat?
5. How were the barges used?
6. Mr. Germain was glad to get out of the cold and rainy weather into the dry, warm lower deck of the yacht. Besides being glad about being dry and warm, how do you think he felt inside about his day with the volunteers at Bellingshausen?
7. How would Skipper Andy make the decision about where the Voyage I team would go next. What was always most important to him?
8. How did commitment and organization play a part in the story of Bellingshausen and the *Anne Boye*?

THOUGHT QUESTION!

Think of a time when you were committed to getting a project done.
What was the project and what was your part in accomplishing your goal?

ACTIVITIES:

VOCABULARY MATCH-UP:
Match the vocabulary words with their definitions.   *(See activity page.)*

MAP STUDY:
Find the following location on a map: Denmark

TARGETING YOUR GOALS:
Focusing on commitment   *(See activity page.)*

GET ORGANIZED:
Organizing thoughts, materials and time   *(See activity page.)*

Commitment and Organization

VOCABULARY MATCH-UP

MATCH THE VOCABULARY WORDS WITH THEIR DEFINITIONS

Vocabulary Words

_____ organization	_____ immense	_____ abandoned
_____ commitment	_____ dismantled	_____ metallic
_____ debris	_____ southerly	_____ torch
_____ embedded	_____ military	_____ barge
_____ waste	_____ vehicles	_____ Danish
_____ accomplished	_____ various	_____ rubbish

Definitions

A. trash or junk
B. any devices (tools or machines) used for carrying passengers or goods, especially ones traveling on land
C. given up completely, left for good, or left in a heartless or unfeeling way
D. generally, toward the south
E. set in firmly or fixed in place, or not easily moved
F. planning and arranging things in an orderly way
G. made up of or having metal
H. enormous, huge, or great
I. of different kinds or several
J. broken pieces or rubbish
K. having to do with war or the armed forces
L. carried out, completed, or finished
M. pledge or promise seen or regarded as a serious responsibility
N. boat with a flat bottom used for carrying freight
O. materials which are discarded or thrown away as useless
P. device or tool that gives off a hot flame
Q. of, from, or relating to Denmark
R. taken apart

Commitment and Organization

TARGETING YOUR GOALS

It is important to set goals and commit yourself to accomplishing these goals.

Give brief answers to the following questions:

I. WHAT IS A GOAL YOU CAN SET FOR YOURSELF IN SCHOOL?

WHAT ARE THREE THINGS YOU CAN DO TO REACH THIS GOAL?

1.

2.

3.

II. WHAT IS A GOAL YOU CAN SET FOR YOURSELF AT HOME?

WHAT ARE THREE THINGS YOU CAN DO TO REACH THIS GOAL?

1.

2.

3.

Commitment and Organization

GET ORGANIZED

What would you need to do to organize your thoughts, materials, and/or time in the following situations?

1. Organizing your desk at school

2. Completing your classwork

3. Completing your homework

4. Getting exercise

5. Eating a healthy diet

6. Getting ready for school

7. Getting to school on time

Commitment and Organization

GLOSSARY
Commitment and Organization
Bellingshausen and the Anne Boye

organization — *planning and arranging things in an orderly way*

commitment — *pledge or promise seen or regarded as a serious responsibility*

debris — *broken pieces or rubbish*

embedded — *set in firmly, fixed in place, or not easily moved*

waste — *materials which are discarded or thrown away as useless*

accomplished — *carried out, completed, or finished*

immense — *enormous, huge, or great*

dismantled — *taken apart*

Danish — *of, from, or relating to Denmark*

rubbish — *trash or junk*

military — *having to do with war or the armed forces*

vehicles — *any devices (tools or machines) used for carrying passengers or goods, especially ones traveling on land*

various— *of different kinds or several*

abandoned — *given up completely, left for good, or left in a heartless or unfeeling way*

metallic — *made up of or having metal*

torch — *device or tool that gives off a hot flame*

barge — *boat with a flat bottom used for carrying freight and or goods*

southerly — *generally, toward the south*

It is not how much we do,
but how much love we put into the doing.
It is not how much we give,
but how much love we put into the giving.

—*Mother Teresa*

Focus and Helpfulness

HALF MOON ISLAND

Mr. Germain got out of his warm cot-sized bed, put on his foulies, and went up to the deck. It was his turn to keep watch for icebergs and ever-changing winds. It was cold and the water was choppy, but his assignment was memorable for other reasons. Toward the end of his watch, Antarctica's crescent-shaped Half Moon Island came into view. The gorgeous approach to land and huge glaciers getting closer and closer was a sequence of magnified beauty. For those moments, he forgot the cold and the choppy water.

Fresh air on deck and keeping his eyes on the horizon, followed by a short nap, eased the momentary seasickness Mr. Germain felt during the morning. After some hot drinks, the Voyage I team split into two groups and went ashore to look at the wildlife. Mr. Germain's first look at a rookery was practically mystical! There were mostly chinstrap penguins with a few gentoos scattered here and there. These are somewhat peculiar creatures, at once stately and comical. What got to him in particular was the way the penguins were spread out over the terrain ... some on the beach at the water's edge, a scattered few halfway up toward the high peak of land but then crowded at the craggy top. Making strange penguin sounds, some in

Focus and Helpfulness

unison, they aimed their beaks at the sky and let loose cries to the heavens! They were completely unafraid of the team members, allowing them to get close for some spectacular photos. Although strong, the odor was not as bad as Mr. Germain had been led to expect, but it was a slippery walk in the guano. He fell flat on his back, luckily not in the guano but on the rocky beach, no doubt as a result of the guano on his boat boots!

During the day, Misja and Peter, the expedition leader, spotted a penguin that seemed to have a piece of netting or wire around its neck. They decided to act as life-savers and wrestled the penguin to remove the wire. To their surprise, they discovered that the wire was actually a piece of seaweed! The penguin seemed none too pleased with them, and they felt a bit foolish!

Mr. Germain felt fortunate that Peter, the team leader, was in his group. He was able to learn much about the birds during this excursion. His group was able to see eight out of the possible seventeen species of Antarctic birds, including Antarctic terns, skuas, Wilson storm petrels, blue-eyed shags, and giant petrels. Peter explained the important role that krill play as the main food source in the Antarctic food chain. Without krill, there would be no birds. Mr. Germain paid attention to the blue-eyed shags, which are flying birds. They eat their food and regurgitate it into the young birds' mouths in order to feed them. He especially paid attention to a certain tern that attacked him when he got too close to its nest! There was so much to see and so much to learn. Mr. Germain was hoping that his meager photographic skills captured some of the wonder that was all around him.

Focus and Helpfulness

DISCUSSION QUESTIONS:

1. What was Mr. Germain doing when he kept watch up on the deck? Why was it so important that he focus on what he was doing?
2. Mr. Germain felt seasick at one point. How do you think he felt? What did he do to help the seasick feeling?
3. Mr. Germain thought the penguins looked "stately and comical." How would you describe what he thought they looked like?
4. Describe the following statement about the penguin sounds: "... aimed their beaks at the sky and let loose cries to the heavens!"
5. Why did Misja and Peter feel foolish when they went to help the penguin that was caught in the "wire?"
6. Why did Mr. Germain feel fortunate that Peter was in his group when he saw all of the different kinds of birds?
7. What important role do krill play in Antarctica?
8. What happened when Mr. Germain got too close to a tern's nest?
9. Mr. Germain felt he had "meager photographic skills." What do you think he meant by this? Why might the "wonder that was all around him" make him feel that way?

THOUGHT QUESTION!

Think of a time you were helpful to someone else. What was the situation? How did you feel? Think of a time when someone else was helpful to you. How did it make you feel?

ACTIVITIES:

VOCABULARY MATCH-UP:
Match the vocabulary words with their definitions. *(See activity page.)*

KRILL—THE ANTARCTIC FOOD CHAIN:
See Fact Sheet — Appendix D

USING TIME WISELY:
Teacher/Adult Activity: Using time wisely means staying focused. *(See activity page.)*

HELPFULNESS:
Define positive character values in terms of self and others. *(See activity page.)*

Focus and Helpfulness

VOCABULARY MATCH-UP

MATCH THE VOCABULARY WORDS WITH THEIR DEFINITIONS
Vocabulary Words

_____ focus	_____ mystical	_____ guano
_____ cot	_____ peculiar	_____ seaweed
_____ memorable	_____ stately	_____ fortunate
_____ crescent	_____ comical	_____ species
_____ approach	_____ craggy	_____ krill
_____ sequence	_____ unison	_____ regurgitate
_____ magnified	_____ spectacular	_____ meager
_____ rookery	_____ odor	

Definitions

A. made to appear or look larger
B. singing together of the same note or melody
C. kinds, varieties, or types
D. odd or strange
E. unforgettable or worth being remembered
F. coming near or moving toward
G. scent or smell
H. funny, or causing laughter or amusement
I. to concentrate
J. groups of penguins, seals, etc., or where they gather together
K. not enough or unsatisfactory
L. hardened waste matter of sea birds
M. the coming of one thing after another
N. dignified, formal, majestic, or lofty
O. any plant or plants growing in the sea
P. to cause to come back up from the stomach
Q. of steep and jagged rocks
R. narrow bed
S. mysterious, or not understood or explained
T. lucky or favored by chance
U. having a shape like the first- or last-quarter moon
V. unusual or thrilling
W. very small fish, or whale food

Focus and Helpfulness

USING TIME WISELY

Teacher/Adult Directed Activity

TEAM MEMBERS AND CREW HAD TO USE THEIR TIME WISELY ON THE EXPEDITION. HOW CAN STUDENTS USE THEIR TIME WISELY IN SCHOOL?

1. Have each child/adolescent make two lists:
   wise use of time and *unwise use of time.*

2. Put children/adolescents in pairs. Have them compare their lists, putting the lists together to form two new lists. They must come to an agreement of *wise* and *unwise uses of time.*

DISCUSSION QUESTIONS

A. *What are the wise uses of time?*
B. *What are the unwise uses of time?*
C. *How can you use your time more wisely getting ready for school?*
D. *How can you use your time more wisely during the school day?*
E. *How can you use your time more wisely with your homework?*
F. *How can you use your time more wisely at home?*
G. *How is time often wasted at school? At home? At play?*
H. *What changes would you make in using your time more wisely?*

Focus and Helpfulness

HELPFULNESS

Helpfulness can be directed toward ourselves or others. It is important to treat other people the way we would like to be treated.

Directions: **Complete the following statements that define positive character values.**

HONESTY is the same as truthfulness. When I am honest with people, I _____
_____.

EFFORT means trying hard to do my best. I can improve my effort at school by _____
_____.

LOYALTY is being there when a friend needs my help. I show loyalty towards my friends when _____
_____.

PATIENCE means waiting quietly and calmly without complaining. I show patience in school when_____
_____.

FRIENDSHIP means not only having a friend, but keeping a friend. To me, being a good friend means _____
_____.

Using good **SPORTSMANSHIP** is shown by _____
_____.

LOVE is acting in a caring and thoughtful way. I show love to my family when _____
_____.

NICE is a small word with a big meaning. When I am nice to people, I _____
_____.

EMPATHY is shown towards others when I put myself in their situation. When I "put myself in their shoes," I _____
_____.

SENSE OF HUMOR helps keep a positive attitude in a cheerful manner. A situation when I used my sense of humor was _____
_____.

SELF-CONTROL helps me to be responsible for my actions. Some ways that I use self-control are _____.

Focus and Helpfulness

GLOSSARY
Focus and Helpfulness
Half Moon Island

focus — *to concentrate*

cot — *narrow bed*

memorable — *unforgettable or worth being remembered*

crescent — *having a shape like the first- or last-quarter moon*

approach — *coming near or moving toward*

sequence — *the coming of one thing after another*

magnified — *made to appear or look larger*

rookery — *groups of penguins, seals, etc., or where they gather together*

mystical — *mysterious, or not understood or explained*

peculiar — *odd or strange*

stately — *dignified, formal, majestic, or lofty*

comical — *funny, or causing laughter or amusement*

craggy — *of steep and jagged rocks*

unison — *singing together of the same note or melody*

spectacular — *unusual or thrilling*

odor — *scent or smell*

guano — *hardened waste matter of sea birds*

seaweed — *any plant or plants growing in the sea*

fortunate — *lucky or favored by chance*

species — *kinds, varieties, or types*

regurgitate — *to cause to come back up from the stomach*

meager — *not enough or unsatisfactory*

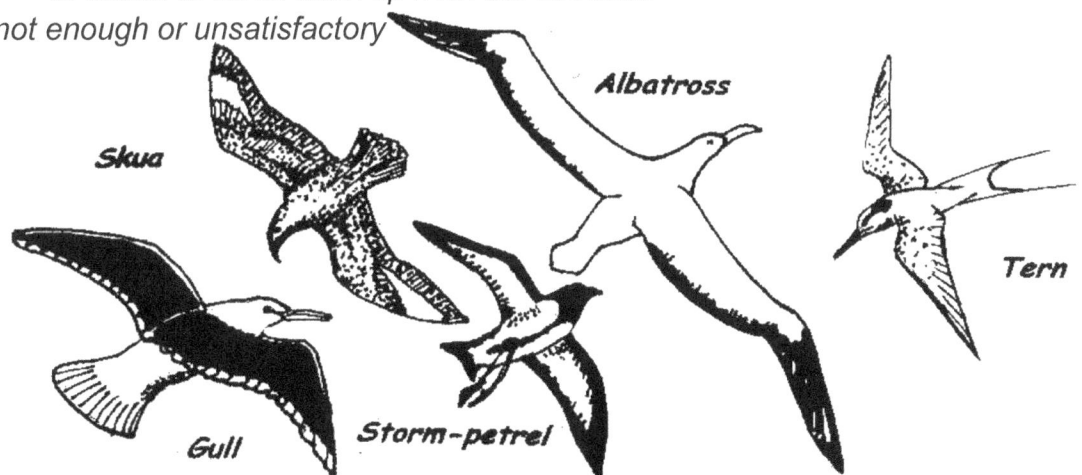

Skua

Albatross

Tern

Gull

Storm-petrel

Focus and Helpfulness

You cannot teach a man anything;
you can only help him find it within himself.

— Glileo Galilei

Attitude and Empathy

VOCABULARY WORDS:	
attitude	rare
empathy	setting
assigned	image
slim	preparation
patient	management
frustration	jolly
reluctant	hearty
decent	content
ice floe	chatting
brilliantly	

PARTNERS IN THE GALLEY

It was Mr. Germain's turn to make lunch for everyone on the yacht *2041*. His assigned partner in the galley was Raewyn, a slim, blond student from New Zealand, who was not used to working in the kitchen. Mr. Germain, as a teacher on the expedition, tried to be very patient. He was at almost a point of frustration when Skipper Andy came down to the galley to tell him to drop everything and go upstairs to take a look at the seals. At first, Mr. Germain was reluctant to do so because he wanted to finish preparing a decent lunch for his teammates and the crew. Skipper Andy practically ordered him to go upstairs, and Mr. Germain was glad he did!

Upon reaching the deck of the yacht, Mr. Germain looked out at the scene in front of him. There he saw pairs of huge leopard seals lazily lying on ice floes in front of a gigantic glacier. Usually the skies were cloudy, but this day the sun was shining brilliantly, adding a gorgeous play of light. The sight was simply awesome! He felt his eyes fill with tears from the wonder of it all. It was a rare moment where sun, setting, and wildlife came together in a most magical way. What a beautiful image it left in his mind.

Attitude and Empathy

Mr. Germain knew that everyone was getting hungry. He could hear his own stomach starting to growl. He returned to the galley to finish preparing lunch. It was easy to tell that Raewyn did not like being in the kitchen. It was definitely not where she had pictured herself on this expedition. Mr. Germain, seeing that Raewyn wasn't being very helpful, told her she could go upstairs and leave the rest of the cooking to him. After a short while First Mate Alexandra, who was better known as Alex, came down to the galley to help him, making the lunch preparation a lot more manageable.

It was a jolly group of people who sat down to eat a hearty meal. Mr. Germain could see that they enjoyed their lunch and he was content. He looked over at Raewyn sitting at the table chatting away with the other students while she ate the leftover crumbs on her plate. Mr. Germain laughed to himself ... Raewyn might not like to cook, but she sure did like to eat!

Attitude and Empathy

DISCUSSION QUESTIONS:

1. Why was Mr. Germain making lunch for everyone on the yacht? Have you ever cooked for your family or helped them in the kitchen?
2. Mr. Germain tried to be patient with Raewyn while working in the kitchen, but started to feel frustrated. What do you think that means?
3. When Skipper Andy came down to the galley to tell Mr. Germain to "drop everything" and go upstairs, what do you think he meant by "drop everything?" What experience did Skipper Andy want to share?
4. Mr. Germain saw the leopard seals "lazily lying on ice floes." When have you ever felt that way?
5. What do you think is meant by the statement: "... the sun was shining brilliantly, adding a gorgeous play of light?" Why did Mr. Germain's eyes fill with tears?
6. What do you think is meant by a "rare moment?"
7. What does it mean when your stomach starts "to growl?" Where do you think that expression comes from?
8. How did First Mate Alex make the lunch preparation more manageable? Have you ever felt like something in your life was "unmanageable?"
9. Why do you think Mr. Germain was content when he saw his teammates and the crew enjoying their lunch? Do you think it was a feeling of satisfaction? Why?
10. Why did Mr. Germain laugh to himself when he watched Raewyn chat and eat the leftover crumbs off her plate? Have you ever laughed to yourself while watching something?

THOUGHT QUESTION!

Think of a time that you felt empathy for another person. What was the situation and what were your feelings?

ACTIVITIES:

VOCABULARY MATCH-UP:
Match the vocabulary words with their definitions.   *(See activity page.)*

ATTITUDE:
Dealing with different situations   *(See activity page.)*

WHAT HAPPENED TO THE EMPATHY?:
Understanding the thoughts, feelings, and actions of others   *(See activity page.)*

Attitude and Empathy

VOCABULARY MATCH-UP

MATCH THE VOCABULARY WORDS WITH THEIR DEFINITIONS

Vocabulary Words

_____ attitude	_____ reluctant	_____ preparation
_____ empathy	_____ decent	_____ management
_____ assigned	_____ ice floe	_____ jolly
_____ slim	_____ brilliantly	_____ hearty
_____ patient	_____ rare	_____ content
_____ challenge	_____ setting	_____ chatting
_____ frustration	_____ image	

Definitions

A. not common or usual

B. more than enough, satisfying, or nourishing (providing healthy food)

C. putting up with annoyance, hardship, or delay without complaining

D. large flat mass of floating ice

E. surroundings, environment, or background of anything

F. way of thinking, feeling, or acting, or position of the body to show feeling, mood, or purpose

G. able to be controlled

H. brightly or in a sparkling manner

I. unwilling or not wanting to do what is necessary or requested

J. given out or appointed

K. friendly talk or conversation

L. thing or action needed to get ready

M. difficulty in a job or undertaking

N. feeling of being discouraged, deflated, or unsuccessful

O. picture in the mind

P. satisfied

Q. thin or slender

R. full of fun or laughter

S. proper, appropriate, or good enough

T. experiencing the feelings, thoughts, or attitudes of another person

Attitude and Empathy

ATTITUDE

Complete the following statements showing your *attitude* in dealing with different situations:

1. When it is time to get up for school, I _____
_____.

2. When I have a difficult problem to solve, I _____
_____.

3. When my friend wants me to come out to play and I have homework to do, I ___
_____.

4. When I am feeling anxious about taking a test, I _____
_____.

5. When I make a mistake, I _____
_____.

6. When I have chores to do around the house, I _____
_____.

7. When I work on a project with a group of my classmates, I _____
_____.

8. When I am angry or upset with a friend, I _____
_____.

9. When I forget to do something my parent asked me to do, I _____
_____.

10.   When a classmate asks me for help in a subject that is easy for me, I _____
_____.

Attitude and Empathy

WHAT HAPPENED TO EMPATHY?

Mr. Germain, a teacher on the team, did not show much empathy towards Raewyn, a student, when he was preparing lunch with her in the galley.

1. WHY WAS IT RAEWYN'S RESPONSIBILITY TO HELP MR. GERMAIN IN THE GALLEY?

2. WHAT WAS RAEWYN'S ATTITUDE ABOUT BEING IN THE GALLEY?

3. HOW DID MR. GERMAIN HANDLE HIS FRUSTRATION WITH RAEWYN?

4. WHAT MIGHT MR. GERMAIN HAVE DONE DIFFERENTLY IN WORKING WITH RAEWYN?

5. HOW MIGHT MR. GERMAIN HAVE SHOWN MORE EMPATHY TOWARD RAEWYN?

6. HOW MIGHT RAEWYN HAVE CHANGED HER ATTITUDE IF MR. GERMAIN HAD SHOWN MORE EMPATHY TOWARD HER?

Attitude and Empathy

GLOSSARY
Attitude and Empathy
Partners in the Galley

attitude — *way of thinking, feeling, or acting, or position of the body to show feeling, mood, or purpose*

empathy — *experiencing the feelings, thoughts, or attitudes of another person, or seeing the world through his or her eyes*

assigned — *given out or appointed*

slim — *thin or slender*

patient — *putting up with annoyance, hardship, or delay without complaining*

challenge — *difficulty in a job or undertaking*

frustration — *feeling of being discouraged, defeated, or unsuccessful*

reluctant — *unwilling or not wanting to do what is necessary or requested*

decent — *proper, appropriate, or good enough*

ice floe — *large flat mass of floating ice*

brilliantly — *brightly or in a sparkling manner*

rare — *not common or usual*

setting — *surroundings, environment, or background of anything*

image — *picture in the mind*

preparation — *thing or action needed to get ready*

manageable — *able to be controlled*

jolly — *full of fun or laughter*

hearty — *more than enough, satisfying, or nourishing (providing healthy food)*

content — *satisfied*

chatting — *friendly talk or conversation*

Attitude and Empathy

What you think of yourself
is much more important
than what others think of you.

—Seneca

Flexibility and Pride

VOCABULARY WORDS:

flexibility	*eerie*
pride	*clutter*
interfered	*vast*
anchor	*cylinders*
lava	*blubber*
ash	*processed*
soot	*didgeridoo*
albatross	*mournful*
dreary	*acoustics*
ruins	*ensure*

DECEPTION ISLAND

Not all things went as planned. The yacht *2041* sailed from Half Moon Island toward Hannah Point, but the weather did not cooperate. The wind was blowing in the wrong direction, which interfered with the Voyage I crew's plans to set down anchor at Livingston Island. The nine-hour day of sailing was long as the *2041* changed its course and continued on in a different direction. The wind led the way to Deception Island, a desolate place that was once an old Norwegian whaling station, and then a British research base which was later abandoned. It was also the site of one of Antarctica's three active volcanoes, which last erupted over thirty years ago, destroying the research base and covering the area with lava, ash, and soot. Steaming water on the beach came from the heat of the volcano. Mr. Germain put his hand into the warm water, which was a complete contrast to the icy Antarctic cold.

It was a beautiful morning, clear with a blue sky. The day filled with wildlife as chinstrap and gentoo penguins shared their space on the ground. Leopard seals and Weddell seals paid surprise visits as they lay in the sun on ice floes. One of the students, Mere, said that she felt as though she were in a movie, and another student, Ghia, said it felt like being in a glass of ice water! In the early part of the day, humpback whales were seen in the distance, and after lunch on the yacht, team and crew members who were up on the deck spotted a beautiful albatross. More often than not during this expedition, the sky was cloudy, so this bright day was welcomed by everyone.

The clarity of the morning somewhat lessened the dreary beach of whaling station ruins that is Deception Island. One of the students, Raewyn, feeling the silence around her, said that if she believed in ghosts, she would say that there were lots of them around the area. Mr. Germain also felt the eerie, gloomy atmosphere of the bay and the abandoned base surrounding them. He wandered around with the other team members, checking out the waste and clutter that had been left there. Vast, circular steel cylinders, in which blubber was once processed, were lying around. This certainly appeared to be another area of Antarctica that was begging for a clean-up crew.

Peter, the team leader, played his didgeridoo inside one of the huge, rusty blubber-refining cylinders. Coming from the hollowed-out bamboo instrument, the sound echoed a slow, mournful song that matched the surroundings of this dreary island. Raewyn, enjoying the acoustics of the cylinder, thought what she wouldn't give to get an orchestra in there!

From Deception Island, the group spotted a cruise ship in the distance. The passengers on this liner were getting a view of the beauty of Antarctica in luxury, far different from the Voyage I group on the sixty-seven foot yacht, *2041*. The team members and crew would not have traded places with the passengers, though. The Voyage I team was experiencing an expedition of a lifetime, ten days of working together; eating, cooking and cleaning up together; having adventures and fun together; and, at all times, looking out for each other. They were proud to be a part of Mission Antarctica in its efforts to ensure the preservation of this continent as the last great wilderness on Earth.

Flexibility and Pride

DISCUSSION QUESTIONS:

1. Why was the yacht *2041* unable to sail from Half Moon Island toward Hannah Point and Livingston Island as planned?
2. How would you describe Deception Island? How did it make you feel to hear the description?
3. How was it that Mr. Germain could put his hand in warm water on the beach when it was icy cold in Antarctica?
4. What was unusual about a "clear, bright morning" on Deception Island?
5. What do you think Mere meant by "she felt as though she were in a movie?"
6. Ghia said she felt like she was "in a glass of ice water!" What do you think she meant?
7. Describe the abandoned base at Deception Island. What kinds of ruins were left there? How did Mr. Germain feel seeing the ruins?
8. What did it sound like when Peter played his didgeridoo inside one of the huge cylinders? Why did the "mournful song" match the surroundings of the "dreary island?"
9. The Voyage I group saw a cruise ship in the distance. Why do you think they wouldn't have wanted to change places with the passengers, even though they were sailing in luxury?
10. Why were the Voyage I team members proud to be a part of Mission Antarctica?

THOUGHT QUESTION!

Andy, skipper of the *2041*, had to be flexible in making his decision to change course, even though he had plans to go somewhere else. Think about a time when you had to be flexible and change your plans because of a change in the situation. What was the situation and how did you feel about having to be flexible and change your plans?

ACTIVITIES:

VOCABULARY MATCH-UP:
Match the vocabulary words with their definitions.   *(See activity page.)*

ANIMAZE:
What you see can be deceptive or fool you!   *(See activity page.)*

HAVING PRIDE IN YOURSELF:
Thinking about others helps us have pride in ourselves.   *(See activity page.)*

Flexibility and Pride

VOCABULARY MATCH-UP

MATCH THE VOCABULARY WORDS WITH THEIR DEFINITIONS

Vocabulary Words

_____ flexibility	_____ albatross	_____ blubber
_____ pride	_____ dreary	_____ processed
_____ interfered	_____ ruins	_____ didgeridoo
_____ anchor	_____ eerie	_____ mournful
_____ lava	_____ clutter	_____ acoustics
_____ ash	_____ vast	_____ ensure
_____ soot	_____ cylinders	

Definitions

A. device or tool attached to a boat, ship, etc. and lowered to the bottom of the water to prevent drifting or movement

B. disorderly heap or mess

C. what remains of something that has been burned

D. huge or enormous, or very great in size

E. destruction, great damage, or decay

F. made or treated by a special method

G. to make sure or certain

H. ability to adjust or adapt to change

I. gloomy or cheerless

J. melting rock flowing from a volcano

K. layer of fat under the skin of whales, seals, and walruses; used as a source of oil

L. sorrowful or sad

M. strange and frightening, or uneasy

N. very large sea bird of southern waters which can make long flights from land

O. blocked, gotten in the way of, or prevented from happening

P. hollowed-out bamboo instrument

Q. how well sound is heard in its surroundings or environment

R. barrel-shaped objects

S. black that forms when materials made up of carbon burn

T. self-respect, or feeling of pleasure or satisfaction

U. to lay waste or make unfit for inhabitants (people or animals who live there)

Flexibility and Pride

ANIMAZE

WHAT YOU SEE CAN BE DECEPTIVE!

Look closely at the picture on the next page showing various animals and birds.

HOW MANY OF EACH DO YOU SEE?   DON'T LET IT FOOL YOU!

PENGUINS ___   SEALS ___ WHALES ___ BIRDS ___

1. WHY MIGHT THE PICTURE HAVE BEEN CONFUSING TO YOU WHEN YOU FIRST LOOKED AT IT?

2. HOW FLEXIBLE WERE YOU IN YOUR THINKING? DID YOU LOOK AT THE PICTURE FROM DIFFERENT ANGLES?

3. IF YOU COUNTED THE ANIMALS AGAIN, WOULD YOU GET THE SAME NUMBERS?

4. WHERE DO YOU THINK THE TITLE, "ANIMAZE," CAME FROM? DO YOU THINK IT IS A WORD THAT CAN BE FOUND IN THE DICTIONARY? HOW WOULD YOU DEFINE THIS WORD IF YOU WERE ADDING IT TO A DICTIONARY?

Flexibility and Pride

Flexibility and Pride

HAVING PRIDE IN YOURSELF

COMPLETE THE FOLLOWING STATEMENTS:

1. WHEN I MEET SOMEONE FROM ANOTHER COUNTRY, I _____
   _____.

2. WHEN I AM WITH PEOPLE WHO HAVE DIFFERENT BELIEFS FROM MINE, I ___
   _____.

3. WHEN I AM WORKING ON A PROJECT WITH A GROUP OF STUDENTS AND
   EVERYONE HAS HIS/HER OWN IDEAS, I _____
   _____.

4. WHEN MY BROTHER/SISTER USES MY THINGS, I _____
   _____.

5. WHEN A CLASSMATE WHO IS THOUGHT OF AS "NOT GOOD AT SPORTS" IS
   PUT ON MY TEAM, I _____
   _____.

6. WHEN A CLASSMATE SITS NEXT TO ME IN THE CAFETERIA AND I WANTED
   SOMEONE ELSE TO SIT THERE, I _____
   _____.

7. WHEN I DO AN ASSIGNMENT IN CLASS OR AT HOME THAT IS CARELESS AND
   "SLOPPY," I _____
   _____.

8. WHEN MY ROOM AT HOME IS A "COMPLETE MESS," I _____
   _____.
   DO YOU WAIT UNTIL YOUR PARENT GETS UPSET ABOUT THE MESS?__ YES! __ NO!

9. TAKING CARE OF MY RESPONSIBILITIES AT SCHOOL MAKES ME FEEL _____
   _____.

10. TAKING CARE OF MY RESPONSIBILITIES AT HOME MAKES ME
    FEEL _____
    _____.

Flexibility and Pride

GLOSSARY
Flexibility and Pride
Deception Island

flexibility — *ability to adjust or adapt to change*

pride — *self-respect, or feeling of pleasure or satisfaction*

interfered — *blocked, gotten in the way of, or prevented from happening*

anchor — *device or tool attached to a boat, ship, etc. and lowered to the bottom of the water to prevent drifting or movement*

desolate — *to lay waste, or make unfit for inhabitants (people or animals who live there)*

lava — *melted rock flowing from a volcano*

ash — *what remains of something that has been burned*

soot — *black powder that forms when materials made of carbon burn*

albatross — *very large sea bird of southern waters which can make long flights from land*

dreary — *gloomy or cheerless*

ruins — *destruction, great damage, or decay*

eerie — *strange and frightening, or uneasy*

clutter — *disorderly heap or mess*

vast — *huge or enormous, or very great in size*

cylinders — *barrel-shaped objects*

blubber — *layer of fat under the skin of whales, seals, and walruses; used as a source of oil*

processed — *made or treated by a special method*

didgeridoo — *hollowed-out bamboo instrument*

mournful — *sorrowful or sad*

acoustics — *how well sound is heard in its surroundings or environment*

ensure — *to make sure or certain*

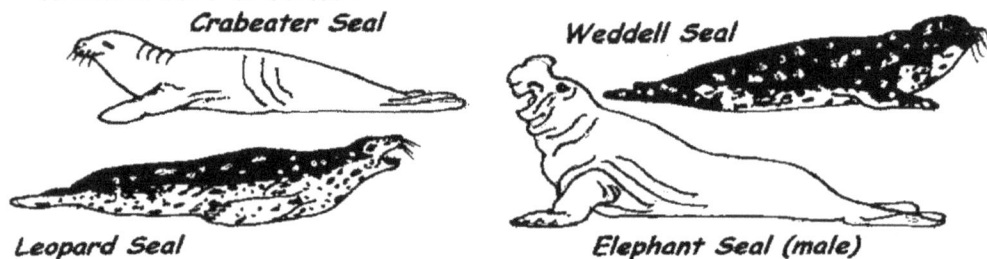

Crabeater Seal

Weddell Seal

Leopard Seal

Elephant Seal (male)

Flexibility and Pride

Flexibility and Pride

*If I have seen further,
it is by standing upon
the shoulders of giants.*

—Sir Isaac Newton

Contentment and Curiosity

VOCABULARY WORDS:

contentment	sculptured
curiosity	landscape
mainland	lounging
prospect	southerly
boarded	unimpressed
dinghy	presence
encounter	posed
calf	basking
ripple	gazes
surface	perched
glory	unique
incredibly	wonder

A DINGHY ADVENTURE - PART I

With the yacht *2041* tied to an old whaling shipwreck off Enterprise Island, the team members could see the Antarctica mainland for the first time. In the morning, the team and crew were divided into two groups for excursions to the mainland. Mike, Alf, Peter, Nick, Mere, Ghia, and Misja, who were put in the second group, stayed behind to give the boat and themselves a good scrubbing. The prospect of taking showers was especially exciting to them since they hadn't had one since they had boarded the yacht. This group would be going out in the dinghy after their lunch.

Alex, Andy, Katja, Raewyn, Macs, and Mr. Germain were the first group to leave the yacht and get into the dinghy for an adventure, and what an adventure they had! Their first encounter was a humpback whale, probably a calf judging by its size, although they never saw the mother. This young beauty played hide-and-seek with them for about half an hour. Although it came close to the dinghy, it didn't cause much more than a ripple on the surface of the water. Once it swam directly under the boat,

Contentment and Curiosity

and they could easily see the awesome mammal in all its glory.

It was a beautiful day, not quite sunny, but very still and incredibly clear. Mountains covered with thick caps of ice and spectacular icebergs with sculptured surfaces formed a most astonishing landscape. It made the long trip into the mainland all the more worthwhile.

As the group entered Bancroft Bay, they met a healthy-looking Weddell seal lounging on the rocky shore. The Weddell seal, which is the most southerly seal and grows up to 900 pounds, was named after Sir James Weddell, who was a 19th century British explorer. Even though this one appeared to be unimpressed by the group's presence, it nonetheless posed every now and then like an artist's model, confidently sprawled, basking in the warmth of the sun.

The next stop in the dinghy brought a pair of Adelie penguins into view, the first Mr. Germain had seen on the trip. They were such beautiful creatures, with a warm gentleness. They, too, were unaffected by the gazes of the group. Nearby, three blue-eyed shags, and later a fourth, perched on a rock for a long while, enabling everyone to get close enough to clearly see their eyes which were a metallic blue-purple color. The unique birds gave forth low-pitched croaks here and there while the team members silently watched. Each new experience brought its own moment of wonder.

Contentment and Curiosity

DISCUSSION QUESTIONS:

1. How did the Voyage I crew anchor the *2041* off Enterprise Island? What could the team members see for the first time?
2. The team and crew were divided into two groups for excursions to the mainland. What was exciting to the second group about staying behind?
3. How did Mr. Germain's group decide that the humpback whale they saw was a calf? What game did it play with them?
4. How could a whale not cause much more than a ripple on the surface of the water? When did they best see it "in all its glory?"
5. Who was the Weddell seal named after? What did this person do? How large can a Weddell seal grow?
6. What is meant by the words: "... this one (the Weddell seal) appeared to be unimpressed by the group's presence?"
7. What was the Weddell seal compared to in the way it was "posing?" What do you think was meant by "confidently sprawled, basking in the warmth of the sun?"
8. How did Mr. Germain describe the Adelie penguin?
9. How did Mr. Germain describe the blue-eyed shag's eyes? What kind of sounds did the blue-eyed shags make?
10. How did Mr. Germain feel about each new experience?

THOUGHT QUESTION!

New experiences can bring a sense of curiosity. What new experiences have brought their own "moments of wonder" to you?

ACTIVITIES:

VOCABULARY MATCH-UP:
Match the vocabulary words with their definitions.   *(See activity page.)*

CONNECT THE DOTS TO MEET A NEW FRIEND!
Let your curiosity lead you in connecting the dots.   *(See activity page.)*

CONTENTMENT AND CURIOSITY:
An Adult Directed Board Game: A "tic-tac-toe" game using contentment and curiosity statements.   *(See activity page.)*

Contentment and Curiosity

VOCABULARY MATCH-UP

MATCH THE VOCABULARY WORDS WITH THEIR DEFINITIONS

Vocabulary Words

_____ contentment	_____ ripple	_____ unimpressed
_____ curiosity	_____ surface	_____ presence
_____ mainland	_____ glory	_____ posed
_____ prospect	_____ incredibly	_____ basking
_____ boarded	_____ sculptured	_____ gazes
_____ dinghy	_____ landscape	_____ perched
_____ encounter	_____ lounging	_____ unique
_____ calf	_____ southerly	_____ wonder

Definitions

A. carved from stone, wood, clay or ice

B. type of small boat, especially a small rowboat

C. baby whale (also baby cow, elephant, or moose)

D. top or outside of anything

E. held a certain position of the body and expression of the face

F. feeling produced by something amazing

G. long, steady looks

H. not attentive, not noticing, or not mindful

I. beauty, magnificence, or pride

J. peace of mind or satisfaction

K. continent or broad stretch of land (which may have islands off its coast)

L. stretch of scenery that the eye can take in at a glance

M. lying in comfortable warmth

N. resting in a relaxed, lazy manner

O. tiny wave on the surface or top of water

P. desire to know, learn or find

Q. nearness of another person or thing

R. one of a kind, or different from all the others

S. unbelievably

T. rested on some height

U. hope or expectation, or outlook for the future

V. unexpected meeting

W. generally, of the south, or located in or to the south

X. entered or went aboard (a ship, train, or plane)

Contentment and Curiosity

CONNECT THE DOTS
To Meet a New Friend

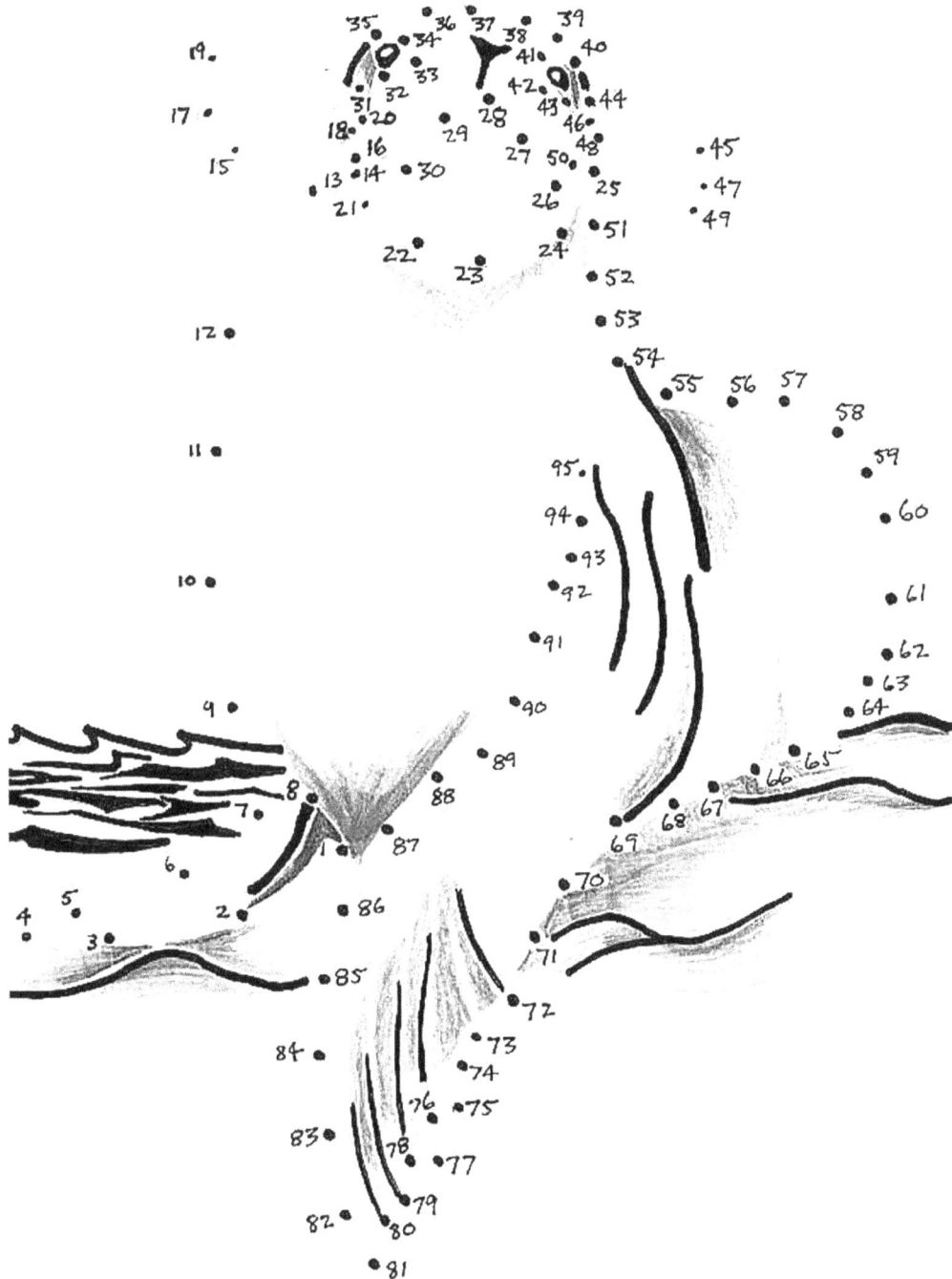

CONTENTMENT AND CURIOSITY

An Adult Directed Board Game

DIRECTIONS: THIS GAME, WHICH IS PLAYED SIMILAR TO TIC-TAC-TOE, IS PLAYED WITH THREE PEOPLE. THE **1ST** PERSON READS THE "CONTENTMENT" AND "CURIOSITY" STATEMENTS, <u>ALTERNATING BETWEEN THEM</u> (SEE PAGE 116).

WHEN A "CURIOSITY" STATEMENT IS READ, THE **2ND** PERSON PUTS AN **"X"** SOMEWHERE ON THE TIC-TAC-TOE BOARD. WHEN A "CONTENTMENT" STATEMENT IS READ, THE **3RD** PERSON PUTS AN **"O"** ON THE BOARD. THE FIRST PLAYER WITH THREE (3) "X'S" OR THREE (3) "O'S" IN A ROW EITHER DOWN, ACROSS, OR DIAGONALLY WINS.

THE GAME IS PLAYED TWO MORE TIMES WITH EACH PLAYER TAKING A NEW POSITION AS 1ST, 2ND, OR 3RD, SO THAT EVERYONE GETS A CHANCE TO BE AN **"X"** PLAYER.

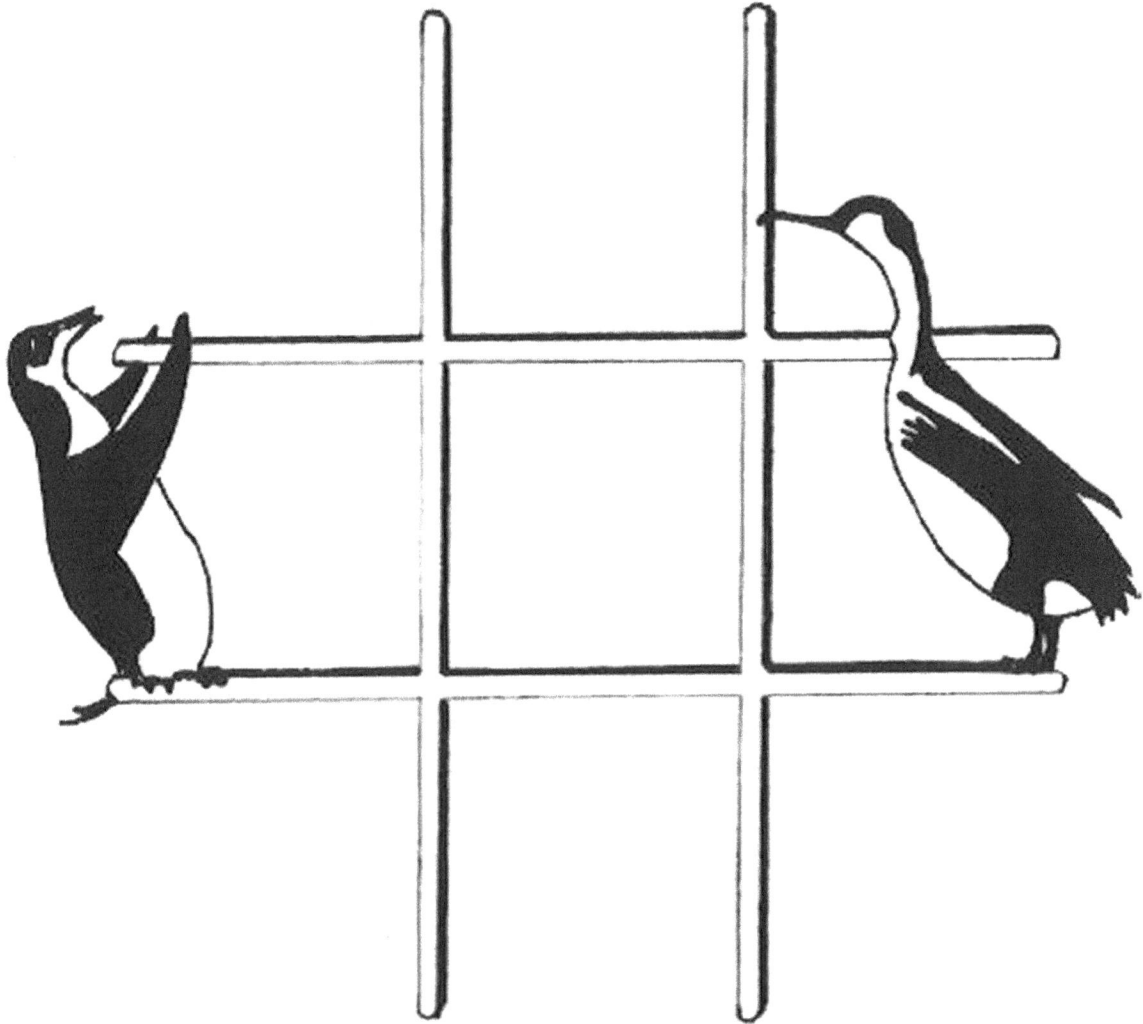

CONTENTMENT AND CURIOSITY

An Adult Directed Board Game

Contentment Statements

1. It was an awesome experience watching the young humpback whale play hide-and-seek in the water.
2. The second group stayed behind to give the boat and themselves a good scrubbing.
3. They could see the awesome mammal in all its glory.
4. It was a beautiful day, not quite sunny, but very still and incredibly clear.
5. The Weddell seal posed every now and then like an artist's model.
6. The Weddell seal was basking in the warmth of the sun.
7. The Adelie penguins were beautiful creatures, with a warm gentleness.
8. Thinking back, I can still clearly see the metallic blue-purple eyes of the blue-eyed shags.
9. The team members silently watched the blue-eyed shags.

Curiosity Statements

1. I wonder what we will see on the excursion to the Antarctica mainland.
2. Do you think the small humpback whale is playing hide-and-seek with us?
3. Why doesn't the humpback whale make more than a ripple in the water?
4. I'd like to know how icebergs are formed.
5. I wonder how large a Weddell seal can grow.
6. It would be interesting to know how the Weddell seal got its name.
7. Are the Adelie penguins as gentle as they appear?
8. I wonder why the Weddell seal and the blue-eyed shags are so unimpressed by the group's setting.
9. I'd like to get close enough to see the metallic blue-purple color of the blue-eyed shags' eyes.
10. I wonder what the blue-eyed shags sound like.

GLOSSARY
Contentment and Curiosity
A Dinghy Adventure Part 1

contentment — *peace of mind or satisfaction*

curiosity — *desire to know, learn, or find*

mainland — *continent or broad stretch of land (which may have islands off its coast)*

prospect — *hope or expectation, or outlook for the future*

boarded — *entered or went aboard (a ship, train, or plane)*

dinghy — *type of small boat, especially a small rowboat*

encounter — *unexpected meeting*

calf — *baby whale (also baby cow, elephant, or moose)*

ripple — *tiny wave on the surface or top of the water*

surface — *top or outside of anything*

glory — *beauty, magnificence, or pride*

incredibly — *unbelievably*

sculptured — *carved from stone, wood, clay, or ice*

landscape — *stretch of scenery that the eye can take in at a glance*

lounging — *resting in a relaxed, lazy manner*

southerly — *generally, of the south, or located in or to the south*

unimpressed — *not attentive, not noticing, or not mindful*

presence — *nearness of another person or thing*

posed — *held a certain position of the body and expression of the face*

basking — *lying in comfortable warmth*

gazes — *long, steady looks*

perched — *rested on some height*

unique — *one of a kind, or different from all the others*

wonder — *feeling produced by something amazing*

Blue-eyed shags

Contentment and Curiosity

...Two roads diverged in a wood and I ...
I took the one less traveled by.
And that has made all the difference.

— Robert Frost

Love and Thankfulness

VOCABULARY WORDS:

love	cavern
thankfulness	fitting
mass	sponsors
necessity	memorable
sheer	astounding
overwhelmed	witness
texture	inanimate
creases	natural
mists	senseless
variations	

A DINGHY ADVENTURE - PART II

Mr. Germain sat in the dinghy with the rest of the group for a good half hour or more in front of Bailey's Glacier in Bancroft Bay, listening to the eerie sounds of the shifting ice. At first he thought it sounded like thunder. Then it reminded him of the sound of an earthquake. After a while he came to understand the sound a glacier makes when it is moving; it is really the sound of the ages of earth. Imagine that this mass of ice and snow that has collected over millions of years moves out of its own necessity, as we do. It was a sound like no other, and Mr. Germain felt his eyes tear at the sheer wonder of Antarctica for the second time during this journey, the first being the sunny day with the leopard seals in front of the glacier.

Mr. Germain was overwhelmed by the beauty of his surroundings. The forms of the glaciers were endless: textures, patterns, creases, wrinkles, mists, chunks ... a parade of natural variations. As Mr. Germain entered the cavern of a bright blue iceberg, Alex took a picture of him pushed up against the roof of it, looking as if he were frozen in the blueness that the light brought about on the ice.

Love and Thankfulness

Back on *2041*, Mr. Germain cooked a very American meal for the first group of hungry sailors: hamburgers, french fries (or "chips," as everyone else called them), and salad. He found it to be a difficult job in such a small kitchen, but he felt it went well and everyone enjoyed the meal. Then it was their time for showers and cleanup! It would have been a fitting end to such a wonderful day, but the day was not over!

When the second group came back from their dinghy adventure, Peter took all of the team members hiking up a snowy hill. It was not an easy climb as the snow was quite wet, but, oh, what another spectacular view! The team had a photo shoot holding the banners of the sponsors for the trip, and all had a good time, as well. Everyone had fun goofing off for the camera and falling into the whiteness of the snow. They were explorers, adventurers, teammates, and friends who had shared a most memorable day.

Mr. Germain wondered to himself: what was more astounding to witness in this environment? Was it the wildlife or the inanimate natural forms? He found it impossible and senseless to choose. He did know for certain, though, that he could not get enough of the beauty and wonder of it all. He thought how valuable a mission it was to keep Antarctica as an unspoiled, natural wilderness, belonging to all people.

Love and Thankfulness

DISCUSSION QUESTIONS:

1. What was Mr. Germain listening to in front of Bailey's Glacier in Baycroft Bay? Have you ever sat quietly and just listened to sounds?
2. What did the shifting of the ice first sound like to Mr. Germain? What did it remind him of as he continued listening?
3. What did Mr. Germain mean when he said that the glacier's mass of ice "moves out of necessity, as we do?"
4. How did Mr. Germain describe the forms of the glaciers?
5. Describe the picture Alex took of Mr. Germain as he entered the cavern.
6. What was the "very American meal" that Mr. Germain cooked for lunch back on the *2041*? Why did he choose to cook an "American" meal?
7. Why did Mr. Germain find it difficult to cook the meal?
8. Why did Peter take all of the team members hiking up a snowy hill? Why was it important to take pictures? What kind of a good time did the team members have on the hill? What kind of closeness did they feel?
9. Mr. Germain wondered whether the wildlife or the inanimate natural forms were more astounding to witness. What did he mean when he said "it was impossible and senseless to choose?"
10. What did Mr. Germain feel was the important part of Mission Antarctica?

THOUGHT QUESTION!

Think of a time when you were "goofing off" with some friends. Describe the situation. Was it an appropriate or inappropriate time for "goofing off?" When would be appropriate times? When would be inappropriate times? (Think of school, home, and play.)

ACTIVITIES:

VOCABULARY MATCH-UP:
Match the vocabulary words with their definitions.   *(See activity page.)*

LOVE: THE ABILITY TO CARE
An Adult/Teacher Directed Activity: Understanding the character trait of love through one of several activities   *(See activity page.)*

THANKFULNESS QUILT:
An Adult/Teacher Directed Activity: Creating quilt squares to discover the meaning of "thankfulness"   *(See activity page.)*

Love and Thankfulness

VOCABULARY MATCH-UP

MATCH THE VOCABULARY WORDS WITH THEIR DEFINITIONS

Vocabulary Words

_____	love	_____	cavern
_____	thankfulness	_____	fitting
_____	mass	_____	sponsors
_____	necessity	_____	memorable
_____	sheer	_____	astounding
_____	overwhelmed	_____	witness
_____	texture	_____	inanimate
_____	creases	_____	natural
_____	mists	_____	senseless
_____	variations		

Definitions

A. feeling or showing gratefulness or thanks

B. tiny drops of water in the air like moisture or fog

C. unforgettable, or worth being remembered

D. large cave

E. something needed, or something one cannot get along without

F. lifeless or non-living

G. businesses or organizations that pay the cost of a program to support it

H. overpowered, or overcome in mind and feeling

I. the ability to care for others, or attraction or dedication to another

J. without meaning, understanding, or wisdom

K. different forms, shapes, sounds, etc.

L. appearance and feel of a surface

M. amazing

N. produced by or occurring in nature, or not man-made

O. folds or wrinkles

P. to see or observe in person

Q. complete or entire

R. main or larger part or amount

S. proper or appropriate

Love and Thankfulness

LOVE: THE ABILITY TO CARE
An Adult/Teacher Directed Activity

Love is the ability to care for others and for the environment. It is a special feeling that helps you to treat other people the way you want to be treated. It encourages you to respect the environment and the world in which you live. Love is a quality or feeling of strong or constant attraction for, and dedication to, another person or the environment.

Directions: In groups of four or five, discuss the questions written below:

  a. *Choose a recorder and a spokesperson for each group*
  b. *Instruct the recorder to neatly write down all of the thoughts of the group.*
  c. *Following the small group discussions, ask the spokesperson in each group to read the written thoughts of that small group to everyone.*

Questions for Discussion

1. How is love shown at home with parents or guardians?
2. How is love demonstrated with brothers and/or sisters?
3. How can you show love to your pet? How can your pet show love to you?
4. In what ways can you show love for your teacher and classmates? Is showing caring and responsibility at school a form of love for school?
5. Can feeling respect for another person also be a form of love? What about feeling respect for your community or country?
6. How can you show love or appreciation for the environment?
7. In what ways did the Voyage I team members and crew show love for the last frontier, Antarctica?
8. If a person does not treat you well, can you "come full circle" in the way you feel about that person if you resolve the issue?
9. In what ways does being loving mean sharing?
10. How does being loving mean caring about other people's feelings and belongings?

Love and Thankfulness

A THANKFULNESS QUILT

An Adult/Teacher Directed Activity

Share this activity with your teacher (or with your family).

CREATE QUILT SQUARES TO DISCOVER THE MEANING OF *THANKFULNESS,* USING BOTH WORDS AND PICTURES. EACH PERSON CREATES HIS/HER OWN SQUARE. STUDENTS MAY WORK TOGETHER TO FORM WORDS. A WORD OR MESSAGE CAN COVER SEVERAL SQUARES.

♥ Through class discussion, list words on the board that students think of when they reflect on thankfulness. Draw out responses from students through teacher's own reflection about thankfulness.

♥ Allow classroom time for planning. Students may work on their individual squares in class or at home. Some words that may be used on the quilt may come from the class list on the board.

♥ The quilt may be made out of art paper or material. After the quilt is put together, hang it on the wall in the office, cafeteria, or library/media center in order to share it with the entire school.

AT THE END OF THE SCHOOL YEAR, PRESENT THE QUILT TO A RETIREMENT HOME, HOSPITAL, OR PLACE OF YOUR CHOICE, SHARING YOUR GIFT OF THANKFULNESS WITH OTHERS.

Love and Thankfulness

GLOSSARY
Love and Thankfulness
A Dinghy Adventure Part II

love — *the ability to care for others, or a strong attraction for or dedication to another person*

thankfulness — *feeling or showing gratefulness or thanks*

mass — *main or larger part or amount*

necessity — *something needed, or something one cannot live without*

sheer — *complete or entire*

overwhelmed — *overpowered, or overcome in mind or feeling*

texture — *appearance and feel of a surface*

creases — *folds or wrinkles*

mists — *tiny drops of water in the air like moisture or fog*

variations — *different forms, shapes, sounds, etc.*

cavern — *large cave*

fitting — *proper or appropriate*

sponsors — *businesses or organizations that pay the cost of a program to support it*

memorable — *unforgettable, or worth being remembered*

astounding — *amazing*

witness — *to see or observe in person*

inanimate — *lifeless or non-living*

natural — *produced by or occurring in nature, or not man-made*

senseless — *without meaning, understanding, or wisdom*

Love and Thankfulness

*If there is anything we wish
to change in the child, we should first
examine it and see whether it is not
something that could better be changed
in ourselves.*

— Carl Jung

Responsibility and Trustworthiness

VOCABULARY WORDS:

responsibility	hoisted
trustworthiness	chiseled
feasibility	dedication
allowance	obvious
considerable	dismissive
potential	earnest
depth	endeavor
currents	illustrate
friction	effectual
disembark	triumphant

ANDY AND ENTERPRISE ISLAND

There was one person who had earned the right to be in command of Voyage I. Andy, as the captain (or Skipper, as he was called) was that person. For safety reasons, more than anything else, this was very important. He made the final decisions on all movements of the yacht *2041*, including where they would go each day, when they would go, how long they would stay, and when they would leave, all based on weather conditions, feasibility, and time allowance. Andy, along with Alex, the first mate, made up all of the schedules for watches and chores. The final responsibility for the safety of the crew and team members rested with Andy.

The entire crew had considerable experience in sailing on the *2041*, as well as much knowledge about the potential dangers of the Antarctic climate, glaciers, and icebergs. Together, the crew and team members gathered at the galley table to help figure out where they were and where they were going by maps called charts. These were not like normal maps; they were highly detailed and gave information such as the depth of the water and the kinds of winds and currents that could be expected.

Everyone on the *2041* took part in the expedition, but it was Skipper Andy who was in charge. Part of the friction that at times occurred between Skipper Andy and Peter, the expedition leader, was Andy's absolute say over everything that was done. Whenever the team was to visit a scientific base, it was Andy who contacted the people at the base by radio and discussed when and where they would disembark. It was Andy who would ask if the base needed anything that the *2041* had, or if the base had anything that the Voyage I group needed that they could trade, such as exchanging food for fuel.

While on Enterprise Island, Peter took some of the team members on a hike up the hill in order for them to take photographs. Mr. Germain stayed behind to rest following an active morning. Unfortunately, the hiking group was late returning to the *2041* and didn't have any radio contact with Andy or the crew. Their lateness threw things off schedule, which upset Andy, who was in charge of making certain that everything ran smoothly. Everyone settled down later and enjoyed the delicious evening ... delicious because Raewyn made a surprise birthday cake for Mere.

It seems that Skipper Andy had a creative side that nobody knew about! Taking a big block of ice that had been hoisted on board the yacht, Andy chiseled a dolphin out of it. He worked on it a long time with dedication and obvious pleasure, with Mr. Germain guiding him through it. The other members of the team and crew were somewhat dismissive of it, but Mr. Germain defended the sculpture and Andy's earnest endeavor. At other times, though, Mr. Germain joked about Andy's attempts at drawing when he tried to illustrate a point about where they were going. Those drawings were not very effectual!

There was an extremely large iceberg very close to the tied-up *2041* at Enterprise Island. Second Mate Alf and Engineer Mike tried pushing the iceberg with the dinghy, but it was too large to be manageable. The harder they gunned the motor, the more they saw that the iceberg was in charge of the situation. Everyone else watched from the yacht as Alf and Mike tried to move the iceberg. It was no use! The more they pushed it with the dinghy, the more ridiculous the situation looked. They never did move the triumphant iceberg!

Responsibility and Trustworthiness

Anchor Watch

- Wake the next watch 10 mins before their time for watch, so they can dress. The previous watch cannot go to bed until the new watch have been to the Chart table for handover
- Be Quiet when moving around as everyone else will be sleeping

Watch Times

WGTS: Raeyn /Basil John

11 - 1230	ANDY + MAC S
12.30 - 2am	Raeyn + Nick
2am - 3.30	Katja + Misja
3.30 - 5	Mere + John
5 - 6.30	Pete + Ghia

Wake Andy If:

- The wind is over 25 k
- Depth becomes less than 18m
- Depth becomes more than 40m
- MOB Range (RNG) is more than ~~xxxx~~ 0.03
- Land moves inside the ring on the Radar
- If the wind changes direction, so that we are being blown towards the shore
- Any Ice comes close to the Yacht
- Vibration from the Anchor Chain/Bow roller.
- Any other yachts or ships come close or moor nearby.
- Ant thing that you are not sure of

Please record the following:

Time	Wind Speed	Wind Direction	Barometer	Depth
2400	8.2	309°	982	33.9
0100	5.8	304°	983	32.5
0200	6.7	334°	983	34.1
0300	3.2	351°	983	33.9
0400	4.4	2.94.°	984	30.1
0500	2.3	333°	984	33.0
0600	3.3	323°	984	36.7
0700				

Responsibility and Trustworthiness

DISCUSSION QUESTIONS:

1. Skipper Andy was "in charge" of the Voyage I. What do you think that means? Who is "in charge" at school? At home?
2. Why was it especially important that one person was in command?
3. What kind of decisions did Skipper Andy make? What kinds of decisions do you have to make at school each day? At home?
4. Who made up the schedule for watches and chores on the yacht *2041*? What is your daily schedule on a school day?
5. What kind of maps were used by the crew and team on the *2041*?
6. There was some friction at times between Skipper Andy and Peter, the expedition leader. Why do you think there was a problem?
7. Why was Andy upset when Peter and the hiking group were late returning to the *2041*? What helped to make the evening more enjoyable later?
8. How did Skipper Andy show his "creative side?" Sometimes Mr. Germain helped Andy and other times he joked about his attempts at drawing. Do you think it was all in fun? Is it okay to joke without hurting feelings?
9. Andy's drawing was an attempt to illustrate a point about where they were going. What did Mr. Germain mean that they were not "effectual?"
10. How did Second Mate Alf and Engineer Mike try to move the iceberg away from the tied-up *2041*? Which was triumphant ... Alf and Mike or the iceberg? Why?

THOUGHT QUESTION!

Think of a time when you were feeling friction in your relationship with a friend. What was the situation? How did you resolve the problem?

ACTIVITIES:

VOCABULARY MATCH-UP:
Match the vocabulary words with their definitions.   *(See activity page.)*

SHOWING RESPONSIBILITY AND TRUSTWORTHINESS
An Adult Directed Activity: Using role-play to show how you would respond in various situations   *(See activity page.)*

WORDS OF WISDOM:
Understanding quotations of famous people   *(See activity page.)*

Responsibility and Trustworthiness

VOCABULARY MATCH-UP
MATCH THE VOCABULARY WORDS WITH THEIR DEFINITIONS
Vocabulary Words

_____ responsibility	_____ hoisted
_____ trustworthiness	_____ chiseled
_____ feasibility	_____ dedication
_____ allowance	_____ obvious
_____ considerable	_____ dismissive
_____ potential	_____ earnest
_____ depth	_____ endeavor
_____ currents	_____ illustrate
_____ friction	_____ effectual
_____ disembark	_____ triumphant

Definitions

A. able to produce desired results
B. lifted up or raised
C. dependability or reliability
D. large in amount, extent, or degree
E. filled with deep or sincere feeling or purpose
F. working at something for a special purpose
G. directions of flow of water
H. possibility of doing or accomplishing
I. distance below the surface
J. cut or shaped with a sharp-edged tool
K. to make clear or explain
L. refusing to consider it or think about it any further

M. able to take charge of, or to be trusted with, important matters
N. possibility of becoming, or possible but not actual or real
O. easily found, seen or understood, or not trying to hide one's feelings
P. effort or attempt
Q. to leave a ship or aircraft, or to land
R. victorious or successful
S. disagreement or irritation between two or more people
T. definite amount given for a special purpose

Responsibility and Trustworthiness

SHOWING RESPONSIBILITY AND TRUSTWORTHINESS
An Adult Directed Activity

WE ARE ABLE TO DEPEND ON PEOPLE WHO ARE RESPONSIBLE AND TRUSTWORTHY. THEY ARE PEOPLE WHO CAN HANDLE IMPORTANT MATTERS AND ARE DESERVING OF OUR CONFIDENCE.

Directions: Through role-play, act out the following situations with two or more people. In each situation, act out how you would show a sense of responsibility and trustworthiness.

1. You borrowed your friend's bike and need to return it.

2. You broke your parent's favorite lamp because you were running around in the house with your friend.

3. You are playing ball outside with your friends, but you know you have a report due at school the next day.

4. A book you checked out at the library is due today.

5. You have a friend who keeps pressuring you to smoke cigarettes.

6. You are taking a test and do not know the answers to a couple of questions. The teacher walks out of the room for a few minutes.

7. You are invited to a friend's house to play. Your parent tells you to be home by 6:00 p.m., but you want to finish a video game.

8. You didn't study for a test and now have to take home an "F" paper to be signed by a parent.

9. You invite two friends to your house after school to play. One friend feels left out because the other friend is ignoring him.

10. You have chores to do at home, but you want to go fishing with friends.

Responsibility and Trustworthiness

WORDS OF WISDOM

MANY FAMOUS PEOPLE HAVE INSPIRED US WITH THEIR WORDS OF
WISDOM. USING ANOTHER SHEET OF PAPER, EXPLAIN WHAT
THE FOLLOWING QUOTATIONS MEAN TO YOU:

"How we spend our days is, of course, how we spend our lives."
— **Annie Dillard**

*"You give but little when you give of your possessions. It is when you give of
yourself that you truly give."*
— **Kahlil Gibran**

"There are no passengers on Spaceship Earth. Everybody's crew."
— **Marshall McLuhan**

"When angry, count ten before you speak; if very angry, a hundred."
— **Thomas Jefferson**

"A journey of a thousand miles must begin with a single step."
— **Lao-tzu**

"Love is the most powerful source in the universe."
— **Dick Sutphen**

"Practice random acts of kindness and senseless beauty."
— **Unknown**

"Be the change you want to see in the world."
— **Mahatma Gandhi**

"You don't live in a world alone; your brothers are here, too."
— **Albert Schweitzer**

"Do what you can, with what you have, where you are."
— **Theodore Roosevelt**

Responsibility and Trustworthiness

GLOSSARY
Responsibility and Trustworthiness
Andy and Enterprise Island

responsibility — *able to take charge of, or to be trusted with, important matters*

trustworthiness — *dependability or reliability*

feasibility — *possibility of doing or accomplishing*

allowance — *definite amount given for a special purpose*

considerable — *large in amount, extent, or degree*

potential — *possibility of becoming, or possible but not actual or real*

depth — *distance below the surface*

currents — *directions of flow of water*

friction — *disagreement or irritation between two or more people*

disembark — *to leave a ship or aircraft, or to land*

hoisted — *lifted up or raised*

chiseled — *cut or shaped with a sharp-edged tool*

dedication — *working at something for a special purpose*

obvious — *easily found, seen, or understood, or not trying to hide one's feelings*

dismissive — *refusing to consider it or think about it any further*

earnest — *filled with deep or sincere feeling or purpose*

endeavor — *effort or attempt*

illustrate — *to make clear or explain*

effectual — *able to produce desired results*

triumphant — *victorious or successful*

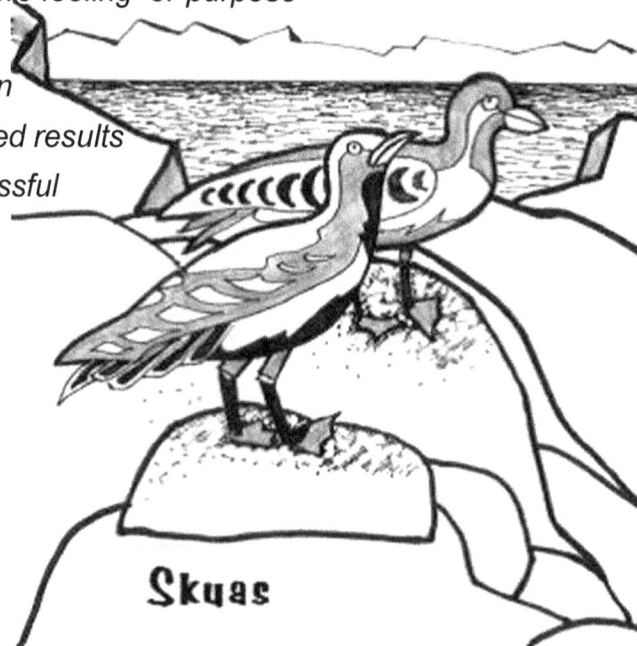

Skuas

No one can give you better advice
than yourself.

— Cicero

Courage and Initiative

VOCABULARY WORDS:

courage	quest
initiative	tow
female	bait
accomplishment	mammals
definitely	snouts
dynamic	broad
duo	varieties
clever	natural
ignored	conceivable
plea	pattern
adventurers	

A WHALE OF A STORY

The yacht *2041* was out in the open waters between landings. Everyone was busy below deck doing chores except for Peter, the expedition leader, who was on deck. Suddenly, they heard Peter's call from above, "Whales!!!" Again, they heard his excited voice call out, "Whales!! Whales!!" Peter had seen a female humpback whale and her young calf swimming playfully beside the *2041*. They all rushed up as quickly as they could, since they first had to put on their foulies, or foul-weather gear, to protect them from the cold. That, in itself, with everyone excitedly rushing around to get them on, was an accomplishment! They all agreed, however, that it was definitely worth it.

What a beautiful sight it was watching the whales spring up out of the clear water and then gracefully disappear again, with their large flipper tails slowly going under. Everyone wanted to get a better look at this dynamic duo, but it was difficult trying to guess when and where they would come up again. Peter had a very clever idea! He tried to get the whales to come closer by playing his didgeridoo! He aimed the hollow-wood instrument down toward the water; however, the whales ignored the musical plea to come nearer to the yacht.

Being the adventurers that they were, the team members and crew didn't give up their quest to bring the whales closer for a better view. It was decided that they would tow Skipper Andy behind the yacht, like bait, as a way of attracting the attention of the playful mammals. Andy put on his yellow wet suit and got into the water. He allowed himself to be towed by the *2041*, kicking his feet and moving his arms, but it didn't do any good. The whales kept their distance. The mother whale was probably protecting her baby by keeping away from the curious group. The team members and crew had to be content with glimpses of the whales' mighty backs, snouts, and tails. Later in the day, however, two huge humpbacks came closer to the *2041*, and Mr. Germain, along with other teammates, saw for the first time how surprisingly broad their flappers were. He thought about the pictures he had seen before the trip and how they did not really prepare him for the real thing. There were such varieties of natural forms, whether in water or snow or air, which went way beyond his artist's imagination. Every conceivable pattern was there in Antarctica, waiting to be seen.

Courage and Initiative

DISCUSSION QUESTIONS:

1. What was Peter so excited about up on deck? What did the others in the group have to do before they could go up on deck? Why was it worth it?
2. Why were the whales described as a dynamic duo? How could you compare it to a child and his/her parent? To two friends?
3. What was Peter's clever idea to try to get the whales to come closer? What did he do? Was he successful? What if he had never tried?
4. In what way is the term "musical plea" colorful or descriptive?
5. How did the team members and crew use initiative to get a better view of the whales? Would this be the same as "putting on a thinking cap?"
6. How was Andy used as "bait" by the team members and crew? Why do you think it took courage for Andy to do what he did?
7. What was the mother whale probably doing by keeping her calf away from the curious group? How does your family keep you safe?
8. What did the group see when the whales finally came close to the yacht?
9. Did the pictures Mr. Germain had seen before the trip prepare him for the real thing when he saw the humpback whales close to the yacht?
10. How did Mr. Germain compare the varieties of natural forms in comparison to his "artist's imagination?"

THOUGHT QUESTION!

Think of a time that you used your initiative to accomplish something that you wanted to do? When might you have shown courage in facing something that you had to do? Describe these situations.

ACTIVITIES:

VOCABULARY MATCH-UP:
Match the vocabulary words with their definitions.   *(See activity page.)*

QUICK DRAW:
Using initiative to copy squares onto a grid   *(See activity page.)*

COURAGE:
Using the word "courage" as a writing prompt   *(See activity page.)*

Courage and Initiative

VOCABULARY MATCH-UP

MATCH THE VOCABULARY WORDS WITH THEIR DEFINITIONS

Vocabulary Words

_____	courage	_____	quest
_____	initiative	_____	tow
_____	female	_____	bait
_____	accomplishment	_____	mammals
_____	definitely	_____	snouts
_____	dynamic	_____	broad
_____	duo	_____	varieties
_____	clever	_____	natural
_____	ignored	_____	conceivable
_____	plea	_____	pattern
_____	adventurers		

Definitions

A. full of energy

B. people who look for unusual or exciting experiences

C. long noses that stick out on animals

D. produced by nature, or not man-made

E. to pull by rope or chain

F. something done, carried out, completed, or finished

G. bravery, or strength that allows one to control fear when facing danger

H. call or request

I. wide from side to side

J. model or example, or design meant to be copied

K. something used to attract animals to a hook or trap

L. girl or woman

M. showing imagination, intelligence, or humor

N. paid no attention to, or refused to see or notice

O. different kinds

P. animals with backbones and, in the female, milk glands for feeding their young

Q. a search or mission (special assignment, task, or work to be done)

R. taking the first step in doing what must be done, without being told

S. two of a kind, pair or couple

T. thought of as possible

U. clearly, or without doubt

Courage and Initiative

QUICK DRAW
COPY THE SQUARES ONTO THE GRID BELOW
IN THEIR CORRECT ORDER

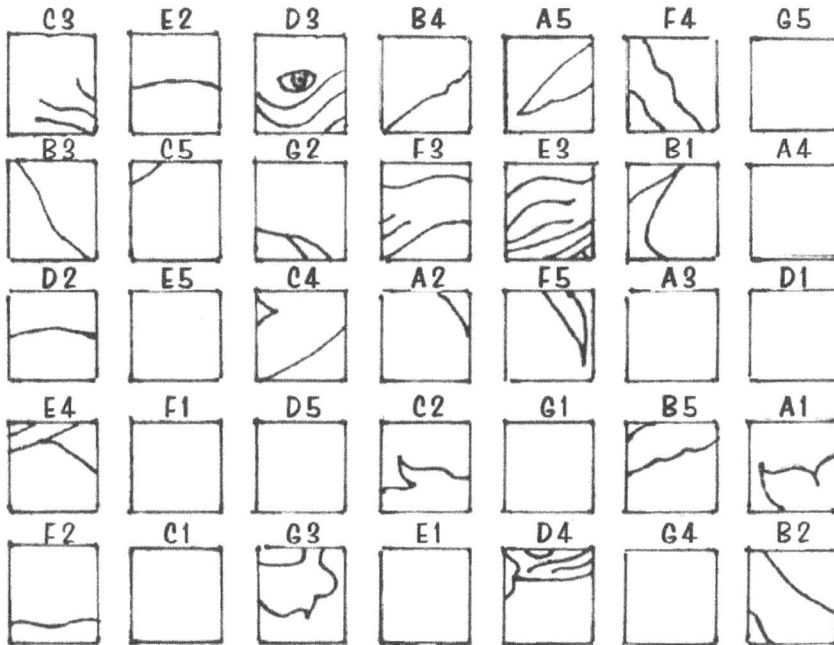

Courage and Initiative

COURAGE

COURAGE ALLOWS US TO HAVE THE STRENGTH TO CONTROL FEAR WHEN FACING DANGER OR DIFFICULT SITUATIONS.

Directions: Using the writing prompt below, write a story about a time you used courage in facing a difficult situation. *(You may add your own thoughts to the writing prompt.)*

standing up to
peer pressure

bravery

facing
fear

Courage

strength

perseverance

admitting
mistakes

Courage and Initiative

GLOSSARY
Courage and Initiative
A Whale of a Story

courage — *bravery, or strength that allows one to control fear when facing danger*

initiative — *taking the first step in doing what must be done, without being told*

female — *girl or woman*

accomplishment — *something done, carried out, completed, or finished*

definitely — *clearly, or without doubt*

dynamic — *full of energy*

duo — *two of a kind, pair, or couple*

clever — *showing imagination, intelligence, or humor*

ignored — *paid no attention to, or refused to see or notice*

plea — *call or request*

adventurers — *people who look for unusual or exciting experiences*

quest — *a search or mission (special assignment, task, or work to be done)*

tow — *to pull by rope or chain*

bait — *something used to attract animals to a hook or trap*

mammals — *animals with backbones, and, in the female, milk glands for feeding their young*

snouts — *long noses that stick out on animals*

broad — *wide from side to side*

varieties — *different kinds*

natural — *produced by nature, or not man-made*

conceivable — *thought of as possible*

pattern — *model or example, or design meant to be copied*

Minke Whale

Humpback Whale

Blue Whale

Killer Whale

Courage and Initiative

Man is made by his beliefs.
As he believes so he is.

—Bhagavad Gita

Courtesy and Generosity

VOCABULARY WORDS:	
courtesy	lichen
generosity	specialists
Polish	greenhouse
rollicking	nudging
fortunate	snorting
marathon	jovial
majestic	spirited
forbidding	animated
hospitality	Tolstoy
flawless	camaraderie
functional	ozone
cozy	cause

NEAR THE JOURNEY'S END

The crew woke up early and got the yacht *2041* ready for sail. They were headed toward the Polish base at Arctowski Station, where they planned to pick up some needed supplies before heading back to Bellingshausen on King George Island. They were only two days away from leaving for home, which meant they had to hightail it back to Bellingshausen. It was nearly 28 hours of marathon sailing over rollicking high seas along with cold winds. Mr. Germain was fortunate on this part of the voyage because he didn't get seasick, but many of the group did. It also was 28 hours of the ever-present Antarctic beauty — both majestic and forbidding — that surrounded them on all sides at all times.

The hospitality at the Arctowski base was flawless. The base itself was functional, cozy, comfortable, and warm. The Voyage I group joined marine biologists and lichen specialists from different places around the world. They sat at a long wooden table and ate Polish sausages and other cold cuts, along with bread, hot chocolate, and cookies.

Courtesy and Generosity

It was a much-appreciated meal for the hungry team members and crew! Their new friends showed them the tomatoes that were grown in their greenhouse, right there in the frozen Antarctic!

A stroll down to Admiral Bay's rocky beach after lunch led to some photo moments with several Adelie and Chinstrap penguins, as well as two huge female elephant seals, nudging and snorting against one another. Their big eyes looked up at the clicking lenses now and again, alert, but seemingly not disturbed. Mr. Germain paused at a directional sign and marveled at the enormous distances between where he was at the Arctowsky Base and various cities around the world.

From Admiral Bay the *2041* sailed back around toward Maxwell Bay and Bellingshausen, the Russian base. Mission Antarctica's Voyage I team had come full circle. It was a heartwarming sight to see more penguins than ever recolonizing on the clear beach. With most of the debris no longer there, the penguins had returned to their homes.

After dinner the jovial, good-natured, and caring Russian crew gave the Voyage I team members a spirited send-off party. Since it was Macs's birthday, the celebration was even more special. There were animated looks on the faces of the Russian men, both young and old. It was like out of a Tolstoy story: their skin was weather-beaten and red from the Antarctic ozone sun; they had creases around their eyes, and unshaven faces. These Russian men were considerate and outgoing. Except for two of the men, the Russians and Voyage I group spoke completely different languages; however, the spoken word was not necessary. Communication was nonverbal and universal in laughter and camaraderie. Everyone was there for the same purpose: to keep Antarctica an unspoiled wilderness and to enjoy the friendships of people of different nations who worked together for the same cause.

Courtesy and Generosity

DISCUSSION QUESTIONS:

1. The crew got the *2041* ready for sail. Where were they headed? What did they plan to do there?
2. What do you think is meant by, " ... hightail it back to Bellingshausen?"
3. Why do you think that 28 hours of sailing would be thought of as "marathon sailing?" Give the negative and positive sides of the trip.
4. How can the beauty of Antarctica be described as both majestic and forbidding? Could the first day of school be both exciting and scary?
5. What do you think is meant by the following: "The hospitality at Arctowski base was flawless?"
6. What seems amazing about there being a greenhouse in Antarctica?
7. Describe the "photo moments" at Admiral Bay's rocky beach.
8. Why did the penguins return to their home on the beach at Bellingshausen?
9. What was special about the celebration for the Voyage I team that was given by the Russians?
10. What kind of communication was used between the Voyage I group and the Russians? What purpose did they both share?

THOUGHT QUESTION!

How was courtesy and generosity extended to the Voyage I team members by both the Polish scientists and the Russian crew? How do you show these character values toward your teachers and classmates at school? How do you show them toward members of your family?

ACTIVITIES:

MAP STUDY:
Find the following location on a map: Poland

VOCABULARY MATCH-UP:
Match the vocabulary words with their definitions. *(See activity page.)*

VOCABULARY ACTIVITY:
Learning word similarities *(See activity page.)*

COURTESY:
Use story lines to better understand the meaning of courtesy *(See activity page.)*

Courtesy and Generosity

VOCABULARY MATCH-UP

MATCH THE VOCABULARY WORDS WITH THEIR DEFINITIONS

Vocabulary Words

_____ courtesy	_____ hospitality	_____ snorting
_____ generosity	_____ flawless	_____ jovial
_____ Polish	_____ functional	_____ spirited
_____ rollicking	_____ cozy	_____ animated
_____ fortunate	_____ lichen	_____ Tolstoy
_____ marathon	_____ specialists	_____ camaraderie
_____ majestic	_____ greenhouse	_____ ozone
_____ forbidding	_____ nudging	_____ cause

Definitions

A. long distance footrace, or endurance (putting up with hardship) contest

B. politeness, respect, or kindness

C. useful, practical, or with purpose

D. people who devote (give selves completely) to a field of medicine, business, etc.

E. full of laughter

F. warm or generous welcoming of guests and strangers

G. friendship, especially of people sharing interests and activities

H. small plant without flowers or true leaves that grows flat on rocks, trees, etc.; made up of fungi and algae that grow cooperatively together

I. of or relating to Poland, its people or language

J. comfortable or snug

K. pushing or touching gently

L. subject that raises interest or emotion, and to which people give support

M. (hothouse) building with glass sides and top that is heated to grow plants

N. lucky, or favored by chance

O. seeming to be threatening or dangerous

P. without weak points or damage, or perfect

Q. unselfishness, or willingness to give and share

S. Russian novelist or writer

T. harsh (unpleasant) noise made by forcing air out through the nostrils (openings in nose)

U. carefree, lighthearted, or without worry

V. layer of stratosphere that absorbs (takes in) much of the sun's intense ultraviolet radiation, thereby shielding or protecting the earth

W. full of wonder due to greatness, size, power, etc.

X. lively, determined, enthusiastic

Y. energetic, excited, full-of-life

Courtesy and Generosity

VOCABULARY ACTIVITY
LEARNING WORD SIMILARITIES

What two vocabulary words are defined as: *full of life, or lively?*
(see Glossary)

_____

_____

Complete the following sentences by using one of the vocabulary words listed below:

rollicking   jovial   spirited   animated

The _____horses were given to the most experienced riders.

The _____clown made the audience roar with laughter!

The audience enjoyed watching the _____cartoon.

The puppies were having fun _____in the high grass.

Courtesy and Generosity

COURTESY BOOK

WHEN YOU SHOW COURTESY TO SOMEONE, OR THAT PERSON IS COURTEOUS TO YOU, IT MEANS THE SAME AS BEING POLITE AND KIND.

Directions:

1. Read each story line; number them in the order they occur in the story.
2. Write the numbers 1-6 in the parentheses at the bottom of each book page. (See the Courtesy Book Layout on the following activity page.)
3. Illustrate each page of the book according to its story line.
4. Cut out each page; put the book together by page numbers, and staple.
5. Share your book with family and/or friends.

Story Lines

_____ Our new friends showed us the tomatoes that were grown in their greenhouse.

_____ The crew woke early and got the yacht *2041* ready for sail to take the Voyage I team toward the Polish base at Arctowski Station.

_____ The Russian crew gave the Voyage I team members a spirited send-off party and, also, celebrated Macs's birthday.

_____ It was a heartwarming sight to see more penguins than ever recolonizing on the cleared beach at Bellingshausen, all because of the hard work of the Russian crew in cleaning up the debris.

_____ They sat at a long wooden table and ate Polish sausages and other cold cuts, along with bread, hot chocolate, and cookies.

_____ A stroll down to Admiral Bay's rocky beach led to some photo moments with several penguins and two huge elephant seals, nudging against each other; the team members did not disturb the animals.

Courtesy and Generosity

COURTESY BOOK LAYOUT

Book Pages

( )	( )
( )	( )
( )	( )

Courtesy and Generosity

GENEROSITY WORD SCRAMBLE

SOMEONE WHO IS GENEROUS IS UNSELFISH AND WILLINGLY SHARES WITH OTHERS

Directions: Unscramble the letters that are in parentheses at the end of each sentence in order to find the word that makes the sentence complete. Refer to the word list below:

forgiving	unselfish	sharing	giving	feeling
mean	friend	caring	helpful	thoughtful

A. Mere enjoyed _____ her birthday cake. *(i r h a g s n)*

B. Mr. Germain decided to be _____ toward Raewyn when she wouldn't help out with cooking in the galley. *(i r n o i g g f v)*

C. The elephant seals weren't being _____ when they nudged each other; they were being playful! *(a n e m)*

D. Peter was being _____ when he called the team members up to the deck to see the whales. *(g u t o l h u f h t)*

E. Mr. Germain's sister, Cathy, was being _____ when she came out in the Buffalo blizzard to pick him up. *(f u p e h l l)*

F. Skipper Andy was completely _____ when it came to the safety of the team members and crew. *(n e l s u h f s i)*

G. Other people's _____ had to be considered while living together in such a crowded space. *(g l e n i f s e)*

H. The _____ nature of the Russians at Bellingshausen showed in their cleaning up of the tons of debris. *(n i g a c r)*

I. Each member of the Voyage I team was _____ of his or her time and effort in being a part of Mission Antarctica. *(n g i i v g)*

J. Peter was both a leader and a _____ to the team members. *(d e r i f n)*

Courtesy and Generosity

GLOSSARY
Courtesy and Generosity
Near the Journey's End

courtesy — *politeness, respect, or kindness*

generosity — *unselfishness, or willingness to give or share*

Polish — *of or relating to Poland, its people or language*

marathon — *long distance footrace, or endurance (putting up with hardship) contest*

rollicking — *carefree, lighthearted, or without worry*

fortunate — *lucky, or favored by chance*

majestic — *full of wonder due to greatness, size, power, etc.*

forbidding — *seeming to be threatening or dangerous*

hospitality — *warm or generous welcoming of guests and strangers*

flawless — *without weak points or damage, or perfect*

functional — *useful, practical, or with purpose*

cozy — *comfortable or snug*

lichen — *small plant without flowers or true leaves that grows flat on rocks, trees, etc.; made up of fungi and algae that grow cooperatively together*

specialists — *people who devote (give selves completely) to a field of medicine, business, etc.*

greenhouse — *(hothouse) building with glass sides and top that is heated to grow plants*

nudging — *pushing or touching gently*

snorting — *harsh (unpleasant) noise made by forcing air out through the nostrils (openings of the nose)*

jovial — *full of laughter*

spirited — *lively, determined, enthusiastic*

animated — *energetic, excited, full-of-life*

Tolstoy — *Russian novelist or writer*

ozone — *layer of stratosphere that absorbs (takes in) much of the sun's intense ultraviolet radiation, thereby shielding or protecting the earth*

camaraderie — *friendship, especially of people sharing interests/activities*

cause — *subject that raises interest or emotion, and to which people give support*

Chinstrap

King

Six of the eighteen species of penguin

Macaroni

Rockhopper

Gentoo

Adelie

Courtesy and Generosity

Never doubt that a small group of thoughtful, committed citizens can change the world; indeed, it's the only thing that ever has.

—Margaret Mead

Diligence and Reflection

VOCABULARY WORDS:

diligence	aspect
reflection	en route
closure	destinations
bizarre	purity
intricate	ordinary
curlicues	vastness
embraces	grandeur
privileged	sacred
intense	regardless
intimate	innocence
extraordinarily	

FULL CIRCLE

It was a time of happiness and sadness. The Voyage I team members had enjoyed an experience of a lifetime, but it was time to bring it to closure. They stood on the airstrip preparing for what would turn out to be a chilly flight back to Punta Arenas in South America. There were tears in the team members' eyes as they said good-bye to Peter, their expedition leader and friend, who was staying behind with the rest of the crew to lead the new team members of the Voyage II. Peter looked rather bizarre in his cold-weather gear and the light green woven straw hat that was given to him by one of the Voyage II students upon his arrival. The hat, like the student, was from Lesotho and looked somewhat like an intricately constructed lampshade with curlicues at the top!

The "changing of the guard" — old group out, new group in — took place in blowing cold rain. Saying good-bye was very emotional for Mr. Germain, especially when he and the other Voyage I team members gathered around Peter in one final circle, giving him a "hip-hip-hooray!" and warm embraces. It all had to do with the very special nature of the communication and adventures they had shared. They all felt they had been privileged to spend an intense period of intimate contact with an extraordinarily beautiful aspect of creation that is called Antarctica. It was rare how it all came together so well, and rarer still that it worked out as well as it did, leading to new levels of experience and personal growth.

Back at the yacht, the Voyage I team members finished packing before getting some sleep, with thoughts of the next day that would take them back to Punta Arenas, where they had begun their journey only ten days before. A stay at the Hotel Cabo De Hornos offered Mr. Germain a hot shower, a hearty meal, and a good night's sleep. The next morning, they all were in the air again, en route from Punta Arenas to Santiago, where Mr. Germain was scheduled for a flight connection back to Miami.

Mr. Germain was going home, but a large part of him wished to continue with other destinations, to wander some more, to taste more of the promise of purity and freedom that is Antarctica. Instead, it was back to the ordinary world, arriving in Miami exhausted from the flight, but too excited to sleep. Sometimes, back at home, Mr. Germain rocked and swayed when he stood, his body still dancing in time with the *2041*, his home away from home for almost two weeks.

Mr. Germain thought about his journey. He wondered how he was to remember the truth that was reborn inside his heart as he returned to his daily life back in Miami. He had experienced so much. He realized that he had a message to send to all people, children and adults alike: *We need to be courageous and make it our choice in the approaching years to strive to protect the majesty, vastness, and grandeur of this last wilderness, Antarctica. We need to work together to keep Antarctica sacred, pristine, and worthy of our attention for generations to come.*

Mission Antarctica has shown what is possible when people work cooperatively together, regardless of cultural differences, to learn about the world and its environment, and reach out hand-in-hand to achieve their goals. We cannot remain asleep to what is possible; we must join together with all nations to return this world to at least some of its innocence that has been taken away.

Diligence and Reflection

DISCUSSION QUESTIONS:

1. Why was it "a time of happiness and sadness?"
2. Why was Peter staying behind with the rest of the crew?
3. Why did Mr. Germain think that Peter looked bizarre? Describe Peter's hat!
4. What do you think is meant by, "Mission Antarctica's Voyage I team had come full circle?" What is meant by the "changing of the guard?"
5. Why did the Voyage I team feel privileged to have been in Antarctica?
6. What did the Hotel Cabo De Hornos in Punta Arenas offer Mr. Germain?
7. How did Mr. Germain feel about going home? What did he mean by back to the "ordinary world?"
8. Back at home, what happened to Mr. Germain at times when he stood?
9. What do you think Mr. Germain meant when he said he "wondered how he was to remember the truth that was reborn inside his heart as he returned to his daily life back in Miami?"
10. What was the message that Mr. Germain wanted to send to all people?

THOUGHT QUESTION!

"We cannot remain asleep to what is possible." What do you think is possible when people work cooperatively together, regardless of cultural differences, to learn about the world and its environment?

ACTIVITIES:

MAP STUDY:
Find the following location on a map: Lesotho (Africa)

VOCABULARY MATCH-UP:
Match the vocabulary words with their definitions.   *(See activity page.)*

PRACTICING DILIGENCE:
Understanding the character value, diligence, through one of several activities
(See activity page.)

MISSION ANTARCTIA VOYAGE I ~ ROLE-PLAY:
Pantomiming scenes from the stories throughout the book   *(See activity page.)*

"PICTURE THIS":
Drawing yourself in an activity and explaining the experience to your family and/or friends   *(See activity page.)*

REFLECTION:
Character Values Scale   *(See activity page.)*

Diligence and Reflection

VOCABULARY MATCH-UP

MATCH THE VOCABULARY WORDS WITH THEIR DEFINITIONS

Vocabulary Words

_____ diligence	_____ privileged	_____ purity
_____ reflection	_____ intense	_____ ordinary
_____ closure	_____ intimate	_____ vastness
_____ bizarre	_____ extraordinarily	_____ grandeur
_____ intricate	_____ aspect	_____ sacred
_____ curlicues	_____ en route	_____ regardless
_____ embraces	_____ destinations	_____ innocence

Definitions

A. constant, earnest effort or zeal (eagerness or enthusiasm), or careful or continued work

B. close or personal

C. simplicity, openness, or freedom from guilt or blame

D. usual or normal

E. side or view of a situation, plan, etc.

F. having a special right or advantage enjoyed by a person or group of people

G. deep thought, or thinking about someone or something carefully

H. curling or swirling in an imaginative way

I. magnificence or impressiveness

J. places to which a person or thing is going

K. hugs

L. bringing to an end, or ending

M. feeling deeply, or giving emphasis or eager attention

N. cleanliness, clearness, or wholesomeness

O. showing no consideration for or care about

P. on the way

Q. deserving, or worthy of great respect

R. unusually, extremely, or amazingly

S. hugeness, enormousness, or immensity

T. odd in manner or appearance

U. complicatedly, elaborately, or complexly

Diligence and Reflection

PRACTICING DILIGENCE

DILIGENCE IS SHOWN BY A CONSTANT, EARNEST EFFORT, OR BY CAREFUL OR CONTINUED WORK. EVERYONE WHO WORKED WITH MISSION ANTARCTICA SHOWED DILIGENCE IN HIS OR HER EFFORTS TO CLEAN UP THE DEBRIS AT BELLINGSHAUSEN AND PROMOTE THE RENEWAL OF THE TREATY OF *2041* AS AN EVERLASTING TRIBUTE TO THE LAST FRONTIER, ANTARCTICA.

Directions: Choose one of the following activities to reinforce the character value, diligence:

1. Interview a parent, teacher, relative, or neighbor. Ask how diligence has played a part in his/her life. How has constant hard work helped him/her get where he/she is today, either in his/her personal life or in his/her career.

2. Write about a situation where diligence helped you in your work in school. In what ways did careful and continuous effort in various subjects help you in improving your work and work habits?

3. Write 6-8 ways that practicing diligence has helped you at school. Write 6-8 ways that practicing diligence has helped you at home. Discuss these diligence lists with family members and/or friends.

4. Write a role-play concerning the following situation; present the role-play in front of your family and/or friends:

   Your friends want you to go outside to play baseball. They insist that they need you on the team because you are a good player. You have homework to do before you go to a Karate lesson at 6:00 p.m. It is now 4:00 p.m. and you haven't started your homework yet. What would you do?

Diligence and Reflection

I. MISSION ANTARCTICA VOYAGE I ~ *ROLE-PLAY*
Adult Directed Activities

Directions: Choose one of the following scenes taken from the stories in this book. Pantomime it in front of family or friends and see if they can guess what it is!

- COOKING DINNER IN THE GALLEY
- MEETING THE OTHER TEAM AND CREW MEMBERS FOR THE FIRST TIME
- LOADING WASTE ONTO THE *ANNE BOYE*
- TAKING PICTURES OF THE ANTARCTICA SURROUNDINGS
- PRETENDING YOU ARE A SEAL LAZING ON AN ICE-FLOE
- WALKING ON DECK LATCHED ONTO THE WIRES
- ON NIGHT-WATCH FOR ICEBERGS AND CHANGING WINDS
- PRETENDING YOU ARE A PENGUIN
- PLAYING THE DIGERIDOO
- GOING ON AN EXPEDITION IN A DINGHY
- PUTTING ON YOUR FOULIES
- PRETENDING YOU ARE MR. GERMAIN DRAWING A PICTURE OF WHAT HE SEES
- WRESTLING WITH THE PENGUIN AND THE SEAWEED

II. "PICTURE THIS!"

Directions: Recalling the stories in *Mr. Germain Goes to Antarctica*, draw yourself in an activity that you might be involved in as a Mission Antarctica Voyage I team member.   (Use a separate piece of paper.)

Describe the picture as though you were telling your family or friends about the experience.

Diligence and Reflection

REFLECTION

A Character Values Scale

IT IS IMPORTANT FOR PEOPLE TO KNOW MORE ABOUT THEMSELVES IN TERMS OF THEIR CHARACTER. THIS SCALE WILL HELP YOU DESCRIBE YOURSELF AS YOU REFLECT ON THE FOLLOWING CHARACTER VALUES THAT HAVE BEEN PRESENTED THROUGHOUT THIS BOOK. GIVE YOUR ANSWERS ACCORDING TO YOUR FEELINGS. BE HONEST WITH YOURSELF.

Directions: After each character value, place a check under the ratings of either **"Nearly Always," "Sometimes,"** or **"Not Very Often"** as it describes the way you see yourself practicing these values.

Character Value	Nearly Always	Sometimes	Not Very Often
1. Perseverance			
2. Tolerance			
3. Confidence			
4. Enthusiasm			
5. Determination			
6. Thoughtfulness			
7. Respect			
8. Sharing			
9. Consideration			
10. Patience			
11. Common Sense			
12. Cooperation			
13. Organization			
14. Commitment			
15. Focus			
16. Helpfulness			
17. Attitude			
18. Empathy			
19. Flexibility			
20. Pride			

Diligence and Reflection

..
Character Values Scale - Continued

Character Value	Nearly Always	Sometimes	Not Very Often
21. Curiosity	_____	_____	_____
22. Contentment	_____	_____	_____
23. Love	_____	_____	_____
24. Thankfulness	_____	_____	_____
25. Trustworthiness	_____	_____	_____
26. Responsibility	_____	_____	_____
27. Initiative	_____	_____	_____
28. Courage	_____	_____	_____
29. Courtesy	_____	_____	_____
30. Generosity	_____	_____	_____
31. Diligence	_____	_____	_____
32. Reflection	_____	_____	_____

My strengths are:

My weaknesses are:

What can I do to strenghten my areas of weakness?

In what ways have the lessons in this book helped me become more aware of my own character values?

Diligence and Reflection

GLOSSARY
Diligence and Reflection
Full Circle

diligence — *constant, earnest effort or zeal (eagerness or enthusiasm), or careful or consistent work*

reflection — *deep thought, or thinking about someone or something carefully*

closure — *bringing to an end, or ending*

bizarre — *odd in manner or appearance*

intricately — *complicatedly, elaborately, or complexly*

curlicues — *curling or swirling in an imaginative way*

embraces — *hugs*

privileged — *having a special right or advantage enjoyed by a person or group of people*

intense — *feeling deeply, or giving emphasis or eager attention*

intimate — *close or personal*

extraordinarily — *unusually, extremely, or amazingly*

aspect — *side or view of a situation, plan, etc.*

en route — *on the way*

destinations — *places to which a person or thing is going*

purity — *cleanliness, clearness, or wholesomeness*

ordinary — *usual or normal*

vastness — *hugeness, enormousness, or immensity*

grandeur — *magnificence or impressiveness*

sacred — *deserving, or worthy of great respect*

regardless — *showing no consideration for or care about*

innocence — *simplicity, openness, or freedom from guilt or blame*

Diligence and Reflection

From throughout the world
They joined to make a difference
One step at a time

MESSAGES FROM THE VOYAGE I TEAM MEMBERS AND CREW — TO OUR CHILDREN AND ADOLESCENTS ALL OVER THE WORLD

"In response to an incredible experience on the Mission Antarctica expedition, I would like to tell our youth to always aspire for more, and inspire others to protect our environment."

— *Ghia*

"Antarctica gave me the satisfaction that absolute beauty exits. Never before have I experienced nature so untouched; what thrilled me was the feeling of timelessness.

"I wanted to scream, Fight! Fight! with the little things you can do to help the environment; then, someday, you will be pleased to see that beauty formed of ice still exists ... that we have not destroyed it."

— *Katja*

"I have learned the true value of following your heart ... if you have a dream and can make it real, do it!

"I will never look back. I have met some amazing people, and done more than I could ever imagine. My life is so much richer for that. I can tell others of this experience, and illustrate why their support is so vital in securing a safe environment for the future of our world. I will carry this with me forever."

— *Macs*

"One step in the right direction may not seem like a big difference, but a million steps in the same direction for the better can make all the difference.

"My Antarctic experience gave me a great opportunity to take my step and encourage others to take that step after me ... a step towards a cleaner, brighter future."

— *Mere*

"Antarctica is a truly awe-inspiring place. It is a place that all of us should cherish."

Amazingly, looking after Antarctica starts at home. Make sure that you and your community make the right choices about such things as energy use, transport,

Messages From The Voyage I Team

and resource use. What we do at home affects the environment in Antarctica and the rest of the world! That's scary, but also it gives you hope. You can make a difference."

— Misja

"Don't let any opportunities pass you by because you are busy doing the same things as everyone else. If you can do something for the environment that makes just a little difference, do it and make a habit of it.

"When you start looking for work, ask your potential employers about what they are doing to help the environment. In doing this, you empower yourself and all young people to work for a sustainable future."

— Nick

"If you have a dream, chase it, for if you fail to chase your dream, it will never come true.

"One needs to come to terms with the consequences of one's actions. Do things for yourself ... nobody else will give you the satisfaction that you can give to yourself."

— Raewyn

"For all of us who were lucky enough to be a part of the six-year plan to clear 1,000 tons of rubbish from the Russian base on Antarctica, it was also an inspiration and a reminder that we can all make a difference in our lives and the lives of those around us by *DOING* small achievable steps of action that assist the environment or help our local communities in some small, but significant ways.

"The voyage highlighted that we each travel a path between who we think we are and who we can be — our greatest versions of ourselves. The key is to allow ourselves to make the journey and explore the frontiers of our souls' destiny. I hope this book has inspired you, and I thank Roxanne and John for putting it all together."

Best wishes,

Peter Malcolm, Expedition Leader for Mission Antarctica/Inspira!

Messages From The Voyage I Team

In Memorium:

Peter Malcolm 1956 – 2009 Activist, Environmentalist, Visionary
Peter *"became involved in a plan to walk to the South Pole. He managed the purchase and re-fit of a North Sea trawler for the task. A group led by Robert Swan, a longtime friend, reached the pole but the ship was crushed by ice and lost even as Rob's team radioed their success. Peter and his mates were left stranded on the sea ice. This was the first of 19 expeditions that took him to Antarctica over a period of 30 years. His work there included service as helicopter pilot with *Greenpeace, and expedition leader for both 2041 and **Aurora Expeditions. His passion for and knowledge of the ice was an inspiration for thousands of visitors he guided to the Antarctic Peninsula."*

Garry McKechnie

Greenpeace is the largest independent direct-action environmental organization in the world. It is an organization that defends the natural world and promotes peace by investigating, exposing and confronting environmental abuse, and championing environmentally responsible solutions.

**Aurora Expeditions believes that travel to remote destinations can create lifelong ambassadors for environmental protection. Sensitivity to environmental considerations is a core part of their culture, and their staff have a unique ability to share their love and respect of nature with their passengers. They take every opportunity to explain the fragile ecosystems they encounter. Aurora Expeditions has been a leader in responsible tourism since the company's inception in 1991. They were the first Australian member of the International Association of Antarctica Tour Operators (IAATO) and their co-founder, Greg Mortimer, is actively involved with its Executive Committee. The Association deals with all aspects of Antarctic tourism, but its most important charter is responsible environmental practices.*

www.svpelican.com.au/pages/peter.html
www.greenpeace.org/usa/en/campaigns
www.auroraexpeditions.com.au

Messages From The Voyage I Team

EPILOGUE

Voyage I had indeed come full circle, but the team members were required to honor their sponsorships and commitments to Mission Antarctica by carrying through with their action plans. Team members returned to their countries filled with the awe of their journeys and a renewed spirit to continue their commitments. Action plans consisted of a series of activities initiated by the participants that were taken back to their communities. Their plans were to spread the word about Mission Antarctica and the cleanup at Bellingshausen, as well as to bring awareness to the environmental issues in Antarctica in particular, and the planet in general.

Each *Voyage I* participant designed his or her own extended action plan, but mainly they spoke to school children, gave presentations, and expanded their messages in newspaper articles and on the radio and television. With the support of his school principal, Mr. Germain offered multimedia presentations to the students at his school and to his sponsor, Citrix Systems; he also added a section to the school's web page. As a part of Mr. Germain's action plan, *Mr. Germain Goes to Antarctica* was written and illustrated as a tribute to Mission Antarctica's *Voyage I* expedition.

In 1992, more than one hundred Heads of State met in Rio de Janeiro, Brazil for the United Nations Conference on Environment and Development (UNCED). The Earth Summit was held to address urgent problems of environmental protection and socio-economic development. This Summit led to the adoption of a 300-page plan for achieving sustainable development in the 21st century. The Commission on Sustainable Development (CSD) was created in December 1992 to ensure the implementation of the Earth Summit agreements at local, national, regional and international levels.

The CSD holds meetings each year that are attended by over fifty ministers and more than one thousand non-governmental organizations, generating a high level of public interest. These meetings help the Commission to work better with national governments and various non-governmental partners in promoting sustainable development worldwide.

Robert Swan, the first person in history to walk to both the North and South

Epilogue

Poles on foot, was keynote speaker at the Earth Summit in 1992. It was there, in Rio, that United Nations world leaders challenged Robert to commit to a positive environmental action involving industry and business and inspiring youth. He was to report back to the World Summit in Johannesburg, South Africa a decade later, in 2002.

Mission Antarctica was the positive message that was born of the Earth Summit in 1992. Ten years later, in August 2002, Mr. Germain and three of his teammates (Nick, Mere, and Macs) joined over forty other people from all over the world at the World Summit in Johannesburg, South Africa. Robert Swan fulfilled the promise made in 1992 by relating the story of the extraordinary removal of over 1,000 tons of waste from Bellingshausen base on King George Island on the Antarctic Peninsula.

The Mission Antarctica team to Johannesburg was composed of forty-five participants from thirty-one different nations, including: team members who had been to Antarctica on the previous voyages, participants who had been with Robert Swan on the "One Step Beyond" expedition, employees of corporate sponsors (with Coca-Cola being the main sponsor), and many others (mainly young students) who had joined the participants after being introduced to Mission Antarctica through word of mouth or through the Mission Antarctica website.

At the World Summit in Johannesburg, a Mission Antarctica "Ice Station" was built at Ubuntu Village as an inspiration to all, not simply as an environmental display, but as a truly unique multi-purpose exhibition and presentation site. School children, young students, and thousands of visitors pledged their support for Mission Antarctica.

Over 35,000 visitors experienced a three-screen audio-visual production of the Mission Antarctica story about one of the most extraordinary environmental cleanups in Antarctic history. The attendees were able to follow the long journey overland across South Africa to the World Summit. They saw a video of Robert Swan and the team's achievements. They became part of an amazing scrap-metal maze and explored South African art projects. They entered a functioning home built completely from recycled waste. They enjoyed the loveLife Chill Area with a water

Epilogue

roundabout that actually pumps water. The visitors took part in the Sustainable Day — how each of us, as individuals, can make a difference in our own lives. They visited the yacht *2041* and shared the experiences of the forty-five people from thirty nations who shared their stories and experiences. "Ice Station Johannesburg" won the award for the Best Overall Contribution to the Ubuntu Village, sending the message that individuals can make a difference.

It was here in Johannesburg that visitors witnessed the beginning of Mission Antarctica's new name, Inspia!, and the forty-five people from thirty nations became the Inspianeers. These names stem from the "inspiration" of Robert Swan and the people who joined with him to make his dream come true, inspiring them further toward taking small achievable steps of environmental and sustainable action. Sponsored by Coca-Cola, all future projects that were to be undertaken would be under the Inspia! banner.

In October through November, the yacht *2041* was refitted for the Capetown to Rio Race. Upon the arrival of Inspia! *2041* in Rio de Janeiro, Robert Swan and the Inspia! team continued to communicate their powerful message across the globe about personal leadership, teamwork, and environmental responsibility.

To continue a "Think Global — Act Local" message, Mission Antarctica joined forces with a local mission in South Africa, loveLife, probably the most powerful organization targeting youth in the fight against HIV/AIDS. In a partnership venture, Mission Antarctica took a team of loveLife groundBREAKERS to the Antarctic Peninsula to share in the celebration of the cleanup. On the return from Antarctica, the team took the message across South Africa on a fact-finding mission to see what people were doing in towns and cities about waste and HIV.

In partnership with loveLife, Earthship Mission Possible was born. The ground-BREAKERS who went to Antarctica with Robert and his crew served as positive role models for youth in the fight against HIV/AIDS. Earthship Mission Possible took note of what communities were doing about waste management and AIDS awareness. They collected thousands of pledges for a cleaner, healthier lifestyle for the leaders of tomorrow, the youth.

Epilogue

In 2007, the Antarctic Youth Ambassador Programme (AYAP) was launched in association with the Antarctica New Zealand and the Antarctic Heritage Trust. The Trust is engaged in a long-term cold conservation project to protect the explorers' legacy: the bases and the artifacts they left behind for current and future generations. The vision of AYAP is to champion renewable energy as their path to saving Antarctica as the last great wilderness on earth. Two New Zealanders are selected annually to participate in and contribute to educate others through their experiences, investing in the future of the Antarctic environment by building capability and understanding in young New Zealanders, ultimately inspiring positive change.

From 2002 – 2007, Robert Swan's dream of building the world's first educational base (E-Base) in Antarctica became a reality. E-Base serves as a resource for teachers and an inspiration to young people around the world.

In 2008, powered entirely off renewable energy, Robert Swan and a small team lived at the E-Base in Antarctica and broadcast to schools and universities demonstrating clean technology and energy saving techniques. During the spring of 2010, in partnership with China Light and Power, a small team lived at the E-Base and repaired damage to the 'Live 365' equipment so that the E-Base could continue to broadcast the message of preserving Antarctica and the importance of renewable energy 365 days a year. A second Educational Base was later built in Pench Tiger Reserve, India, broadcasting their message of the importance of renewable energy.

Twelve nations signed the Antarctic Treaty on December 1959, but the treaty was not implemented. Since 1993, informative meetings have been held more frequently. Additional meetings within the Antarctic Treaty system have produced agreements on conservation of seals, living resources, and comprehensive environmental protection. As of April 2010, 17 additional nations had achieved advisory status by accepting the treaty and by conducting substantial scientific research in Antarctica. Since then, another 21 nations have joined with the Antarctic Treaty agreeing to abide by it. As of 2014, the 50 Antarctic Treaty nations represent about two-thirds of the world's human population.

Epilogue

In March 2014, GEMS Modern Academy, in South City, Gurganon India, created history by being the first school to join Robert Swan's mission to save Antarctica. The nine students selected for an Antarctica expedition are called Buccaneers. This group experienced a two-day summit with Robert Swan in Ushuaia, Argentina, the southernmost city in the world. The group, Leadership in the Edge, then set off for Antarctica to test their leadership skills.

On July 1, 2014, the Launch of the New World, South Pole Energy Challenge took place. Robert Swan's response to the world's increasing energy challenges was working towards developing new solutions to meet people's energy needs while preserving the health of the planet.

On September 23, 2014, the United Nations Climate Summit, one of the largest gatherings ever on climate change, began in New York City, drawing representatives from 120 countries. This summit differs from others with an unprecedented number of companies, investors, and finance ministers involved in fighting global warming. Business has become increasingly focused on trying to be part of the clean energy revolution. Thirty-nine major companies will be joining environmental groups and 32 countries to stop deforestations, which can increase global warming by releasing more heat-trapping carbon dioxide into the atmosphere. Six of the world's largest oil and gas companies are committed by way of a new partnership with the Climate and Clean Air Coalition to take steps to reduce methane leaks in fossil fuel production. United States President Barak Obama told the U.N. General Assembly: *We can only succeed in combating climate change if we are joined in this effort by every nation, developed and developing alike*, adding, *nobody gets a pass*. United Nations Secretary General, Ban Ki Moon, organized the Climate Summit to build momentum for a new international agreement finalized during U.N. talks in Paris in 2015.

In March 2015, United States President Barack Obama ordered the federal government to cut its release of greenhouse gases by 40 percent. His executive order also directed the government to "ramp up" use of renewable energy sources to 30 percent of the government's consumption.

Epilogue

In April 2015, as Chair of the Arctic Council, John Kerry, United States Secretary of State, pushed for a decrease in greenhouse-gas emissions by cities, universities, and other institutions, as well as increased citizen support in reducing carbon pollution blamed for the planet's warming. He plans to use his two-year term to highlight the connection between melting ice in the Arctic regions and environmental effects around the globe.

In September 2015, Pope Francis, in his White House speech, addressed the issue of climate change, stating it can no longer be left to future generations. He stressed the world's responsibility to take climate change seriously, applauding President Barack Obama's legislation to reduce carbon emissions.

The United Nations COP21 conference on global warming, held in Paris, France from November 30 to December 12, 2015, was the largest gathering ever of world leaders. A landmark climate change agreement among 196 developed and developing countries, with emissions limited to relatively safe levels of 2.0C, (with aspirations of 1.5C) was hailed as a 'major leap for mankind' – 'historic, durable, and ambitious.' Though not perfect, the agreement has been acclaimed as the world's 'greatest diplomatic success,' with regular reviews to ensure these commitments can be increased in line with scientific advice. The Paris agreement was the result of more than 23 years of international attempts under the UN to create cooperative action on the global crisis of climate change.

Kumi Naidoo, executive director of Greenpeace International, stated: *It sometimes seems that the countries of the UN can unite on nothing, but nearly 200 countries have come together and agreed on a deal. Today, the human race has joined in a common cause.*

President Barack Obama, affirmed: *Together we've shown what's possible when the world stands as one … This agreement represents the best chance we have to save the one planet we've got."*

In 2015, the International Antarctic Expedition (IAE 2015) took a carefully selected team of corporate leaders, environmentalists, entrepreneurs, teachers, and young people on an expedition. Their purpose was to gain firsthand knowledge

Epilogue

of Antarctica's fragile ecosystem, and acknowledge the wildlife and landscape, all the while learning about climate change and what we can do to protect this magnificent wilderness.

From November 2015 to January 2016, Robert Swan, OBE led 'The Return from the South Pole,' an expedition retracing his steps of 30 years before. His son, Barney, joined him. Robert Swan's journeys included more than walking to the poles, carrying out missions to Antarctica, youth initiatives, and emphasis on sustainability, climate change, and global warming. It involved the difficult and time-consuming necessities of lecturing and fund raising to make his dreams and promises come to fruition. It took confidence, courage, initiative and perseverance.

It's an incredible story, from beginning to present: Mission Antarctica ... Earthship Mission Possible ... loveLife groundBREAKERS ... Inspianeers ... Inspia! ... Antarctic Youth Ambassador Programme ... Leadership on the Edge Program ... Educational Bases (E-Bases) ... International Antarctic Expeditions. It's a story about humanity and changing lives, about individuals who make a difference — a continuous, everlasting journey for the world and all mankind.

"I hope that Antarctica will be ruled by what Abraham Lincoln called "the better angels of our nature." That's been my ideal ever since that faltering promise out on the barrier – to help people to discover that this land that I love is a place that's ultimately worth preserving ... The challenge of modern life is not a lack of information or even of resources. It's a lack of inspiration.

"In the year 2041, the polar regions will be able to tell us if we are saving the planet for human life or destroying it. If in 2041 global warming has continued unabated, the polar regions will be the hardest hit, and we will have failed. If in 2041 the international community cannot summon the cooperation necessary to preserve Antarctica as 'a Natural Reserve Land for Science and Peace,' then we have failed. "My job, and the mission of the 2041 organization, has been to inspire people, to get them to believe that a journey is possible by showing them small, achievable

steps ... Antarctica helps us measure not only the problem of human-induced climate change but also the possibilities of humanity working together toward a solution. The challenge now is to inspire the young people of today to recognize the importance of 2041 as a goal, a test, and a concept."

Robert Swan (*"The Earth's Last Wilderness"*)

Green Heroes: Protectors of the Planet
(TIME Books)

"When it comes to cleaning up the planet, a few smart people with a few good ideas can often make all the difference. Here are some of the best."

Citizens: The residents of Vauban, German

Activists: David Suzuki and Annie Leonard

Royals: Prince Mostapha Zaher and Prince Charles

Designer: Vaerie Casey

Explorers: Pen Hadow, Martin Hartley, and Ann Daniels

Physicist: Olga Speranskaya

Scientist: David Keith

Film Makers: David Attenborough and Al Gore

Inventor: Bindeshwar Pathak

Epilogue

Chef: Alice Waters

Pollution Monitor: Zhao Zhong

Photographer: Yann Arthus-Bertrand

Philosopher: Sheri Liao

Campaigner: Marc Ona

Paleoclimatologist: Lonnie Thompson

Entrepreneur: Shai Agassi

References:

www.inspia.org
www.coldregions.org/index.html www.google.com/search?q=antarctica+pro
www.nsf.gov/news/ipy/Default.html
www.geonames.usgs.gov/antarctic/index.html
www.nsf.gov/geo/plr/antarct/ngo.policy.isp
www.nsf.gov/geo/plr/antarct/anttrty.jsp
www.2041.com/antarctic-expeditions
www.youtube.com/watch?v=zCUe7XdzW0
www.ats.aq/e/ats.htmwww.nsf.gov/geo/plr/antarct/anttrty.jsp
www.usatoday.com
www.sunsentinel.com: Warrick, Joby, "More pressure needed on climate change,
    Kerry says." 4/26/ 2015.
www.washingtonpost.com/text-of-pope-franciss-speech-at-the-white-house/2015/09
www.sunsentinel.com: Lederman, Josh. "Obama orders 40% cut in federal
    greenhouse gases." 5/20/2015.
Swan, Robert with Gil Reavill. "The Earth's Last Wilderness – A Quest To Save
    Antarctica." (New York: Broadway Books, 2009)
www.abcnews.go.com/international-climate-pact-approved-cop-21- conference/story
www.thegardian.com/environment/2015/dec
Walsh, Bryan with TIME correspondents. Global Warming – The Causes, The Perils,
    The Solutions. (New York: TIME Books, 2012)
http://2041.com (*2041* Foundation)

Epilogue

ANSWER KEYS
VOCABULARY MATCH-UP

SNOWBOUND!

___C___ perseverance
___H___ problem-solving
___K___ snowdrift
___A___ expedition
___P___ stranded
___M___ maintenance
___I___ de-iced
___N___ feat
___B___ blizzard

___Q___ considerably
___F___ temporarily
___J___ frantic
___L___ snowbound
___E___ back roads
___G___ diesel fumes
___D___ permeated
___R___ shuttle
___O___ companions

GOING TO ANTARCTICA!

___D___ enthusiasm
___J___ occurred
___E___ continent
___A___ preserve
___P___ generation
___H___ authentic
___K___ festivities
___N___ port
___I___ peninsula
___L___ visibility

___G___ confident
___C___ eager
___Q___ treacherous
___F___ anxious
___O___ gravel
___B___ runway
___R___ crew
___M___ awaited

THE PLACE NEAR THE BOTTOM OF THE WORLD

___K___ symbolic
___D___ remarkable
___I___ friction
___O___ miraculous
___F___ terrain
___S___ composed
___C___ excursion
___N___ keenly
___Q___ endanger
___H___ anticipation

___T___ insecure
___G___ barge
___E___ freighter
___M___ eventual
___R___ recycling
___A___ pristine
___J___ determination
___P___ novel
___B___ tolerance
___L___ customs

SHARING SPACE

__C__ sharing
__K__ respect
__I__ refitted
__M__ rigorous
__B__ impression
__G__ surroundings
__N__ pitched
__F__ secured

__H__ privacy
__O__ scarce
__A__ galley
__P__ quarters
__E__ cramped
__J__ tours
__L__ adjusting
__D__ expectant

FOULIES

__I__ patience
__A__ cumbersome
__P__ gear
__E__ foul-weather
__L__ outerwear
__G__ feat
__K__ suspenders
__B__ vest
__H__ soles

__O__ protection
__C__ balm
__F__ bulky
__N__ rigors
__J__ long-john
__D__ considerate
__Q__ former
__M__ luxury

LESSONS LEARNED

__F__ common sense
__L__ cooperation
__J__ glacier
__C__ awesome
__P__ iceberg
__S__ logical
__E__ factual
__V__ grasp
__R__ concepts
__H__ envied
__O__ glimpse

__G__ aspect
__B__ emphasized
__T__ procedures
__I__ discarding
__D__ biodegradable
__M__ hefty
__A__ litter
__Q__ unstable
__K__ radar
__N__ forged
__U__ displayed

BELLINGSHAUSEN AND THE ANNE BOYE

__F__	organization	__N__	dismantled	__P__	torch
__M__	commitment	__D__	southerly	__H__	barge
__J__	debris	__K__	military	__Q__	Danish
__E__	embedded	__B__	vehicles	__A__	rubbish
__O__	waste	__I__	various		
__L__	accomplished	__C__	abandoned		
__R__	immense	__G__	metallic		

HALF MOON ISLAND

__I__	focus	__D__	peculiar	__T__	fortunate
__R__	cot	__N__	stately	__C__	species
__E__	memorable	__H__	comical	__W__	krill
__U__	crescent	__Q__	craggy	__P__	regurgitate
__F__	approach	__B__	unison	__K__	meager
__M__	sequence	__V__	spectacular		
__A__	magnified	__G__	odor		
__J__	rookery	__L__	guano		
__S__	mystical	__O__	seaweed		

PARTNERS IN THE GALLEY

__F__	attitude	__I__	reluctant	__L__	preparation
__T__	empathy	__S__	decent	__G__	management
__J__	assigned	__D__	ice floe	__R__	jolly
__Q__	slim	__H__	brilliantly	__B__	hearty
__C__	patient	__A__	rare	__P__	content
__M__	challenge	__E__	setting	__K__	chatting
__N__	frustration	__O__	image		

Appendix A

DECEPTION ISLAND

__H__ flexibility	__N__ albatross	__K__ blubber
__T__ pride	__I__ dreary	__F__ processed
__O__ interfered	__E__ ruins	__P__ didgeridoo
__A__ anchor	__M__ eerie	__L__ mournful
__J__ lava	__B__ clutter	__Q__ acoustics
__C__ ash	__D__ vast	__G__ ensure
__S__ soot	__R__ cylinders	

A DINGHY ADVENTURE - PART I

__J__ contentment	__O__ ripple	__H__ unimpressed
__P__ curiosity	__D__ surface	__Q__ presence
__K__ mainland	__I__ glory	__E__ posed
__U__ prospect	__S__ incredibly	__M__ basking
__X__ boarded	__A__ sculptured	__G__ gazes
__B__ dinghy	__L__ landscape	__T__ perched
__V__ encounter	__N__ lounging	__R__ unique
__C__ calf	__W__ southerly	__F__ wonder

A DINGHY ADVENTURE - PART II

__I__ love	__D__ cavern
__A__ thankfulness	__S__ fitting
__R__ mass	__G__ sponsors
__E__ necessity	__C__ memorable
__Q__ sheer	__M__ astounding
__H__ overwhelmed	__P__ witness
__L__ texture	__F__ inanimate
__O__ creases	__N__ natural
__B__ mists	__J__ senseless
__K__ variations	

Appendix A

ANDY AND ENTERPRISE ISLAND

__M__	responsibility		__B__	hoisted
__C__	trustworthiness		__J__	chiseled
__H__	feasibility		__F__	dedication
__T__	allowance		__O__	obvious
__D__	considerable		__L__	dismissive
__N__	potential		__E__	earnest
__I__	depth		__P__	endeavor
__G__	currents		__K__	illustrate
__S__	friction		__A__	effectual
__Q__	disembark		__R__	triumphant

A WHALE OF A STORY

__G__	courage		__Q__	quest
__R__	initiative		__E__	tow
__L__	female		__K__	bait
__F__	accomplishment		__P__	mammals
__U__	definitely		__C__	snouts
__A__	dynamic		__I__	broad
__S__	duo		__O__	varieties
__M__	clever		__D__	natural
__N__	ignored		__T__	conceivable
__H__	plea		__J__	pattern
__B__	adventurers			

NEAR THE JOURNEY'S END

___B___ courtesy
___Q___ generosity
___I___ Polish
___U___ rollicking
___T___ fortunate
___N___ marathon
___W___ majestic
___O___ forbidding

___F___ hospitality
___P___ flawless
___C___ functional
___J___ cozy
___H___ lichen
___D___ specialists
___M___ greenhouse
___K___ nudging

___T___ snorting
___E___ jovial
___Y___ spirited
___X___ animated
___S___ Tolstoy
___G___ camaraderie
___U___ ozone
___L___ cause

FULL CIRCLE

___A___ diligence
___G___ reflection
___L___ closure
___T___ bizarre
___U___ intricate
___H___ curlicues
___K___ embraces

___F___ privileged
___M___ intense
___B___ intimate
___R___ extraordinarily
___E___ aspect
___P___ enroute
___J___ destinations

___N___ purity
___D___ ordinary
___S___ vastness
___I___ grandeur
___Q___ sacred
___O___ regardless
___C___ innocence

INSIDE THE 2041
ANSWER KEY

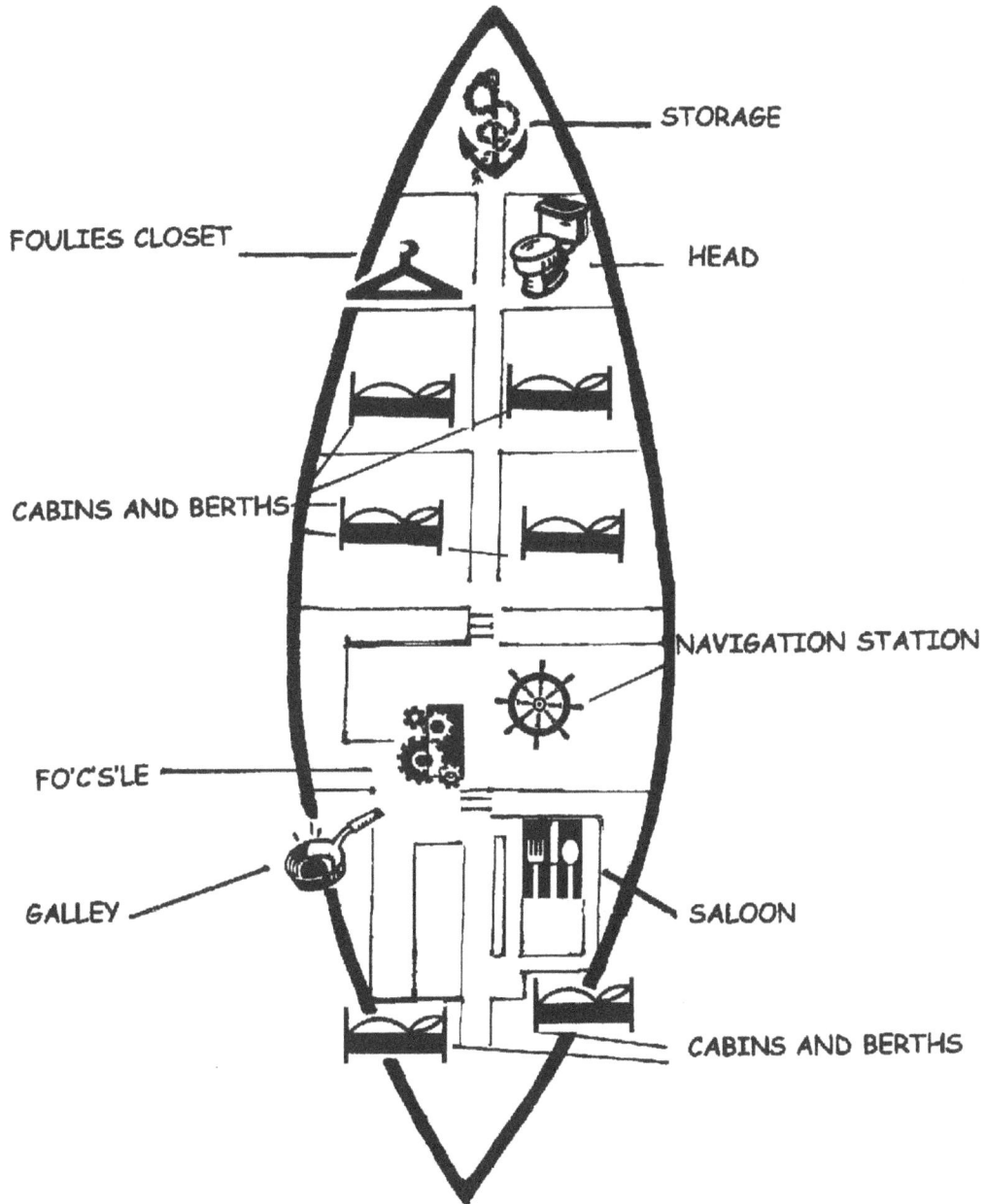

STORAGE

FOULIES CLOSET

HEAD

CABINS AND BERTHS

NAVIGATION STATION

FO'C'S'LE

GALLEY

SALOON

CABINS AND BERTHS

GET YOUR FOULIES ON!
ANSWER KEY

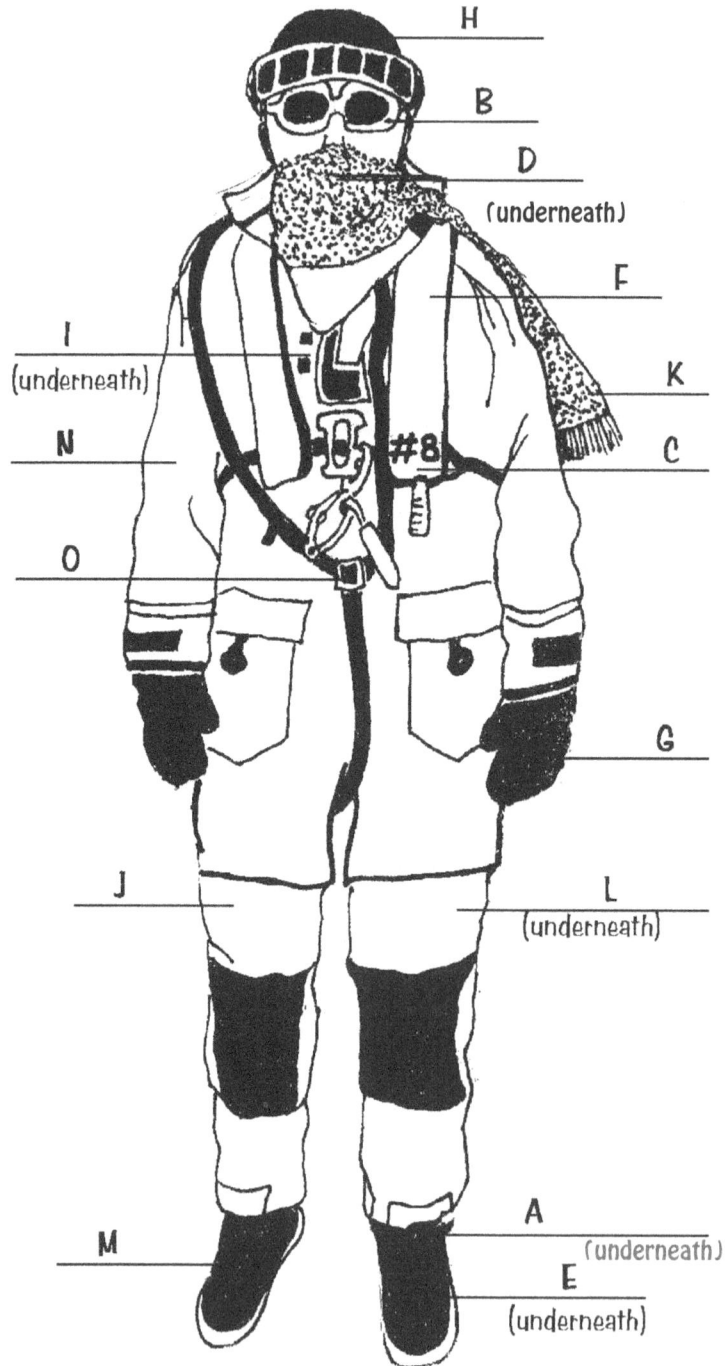

Appendix A

WORD SEARCH
ANSWER KEY

O	U	T	R	A	D	I	S	C	A	R	D	I	N	G	B	A
L	C	F	F	C	O	O	P	E	R	A	T	I	O	N	U	L
F	O	A	T	G	N	P	B	T	W	L	G	R	A	S	P	N
B	M	C	P	R	O	C	E	D	U	R	E	S	M	T	J	C
I	M	T	D	F	W	P	E	B	K	L	O	G	I	C	A	L
O	O	U	P	U	Q	I	R	T	C	F	U	L	K	M	R	J
D	N	A	B	U	V	K	G	O	S	W	T	A	Z	B	D	G
E	S	L	I	N	D	N	L	P	C	O	N	C	E	P	T	S
G	E	C	E	S	I	M	I	O	A	K	M	I	Q	H	I	K
R	N	I	I	T	S	G	M	U	N	A	H	E	L	E	I	M
A	S	T	C	A	P	E	P	R	A	D	A	R	A	F	T	Z
D	E	T	E	B	L	J	S	A	F	I	P	E	L	T	L	E
A	Z	T	B	L	A	W	E	S	O	M	E	G	R	Y	S	F
B	M	E	E	E	Y	R	M	K	R	G	L	I	M	R	S	A
L	W	R	R	O	E	E	L	O	G	I	M	A	U	K	E	C
E	A	D	G	F	D	S	O	R	E	L	P	O	R	C	E	T
E	M	P	H	A	S	I	Z	E	D	M	C	P	G	L	A	U

Vocabulary Words

common sense	concepts	litter
cooperation	envied	unstable
glacier	glimpse	radar
awesome	emphasized	forged
iceberg	procedures	course
logical	discarding	displayed
factual	biodegradable	
grasp	hefty	

SAILING ... A NEW LANGUAGE
ANSWER KEY

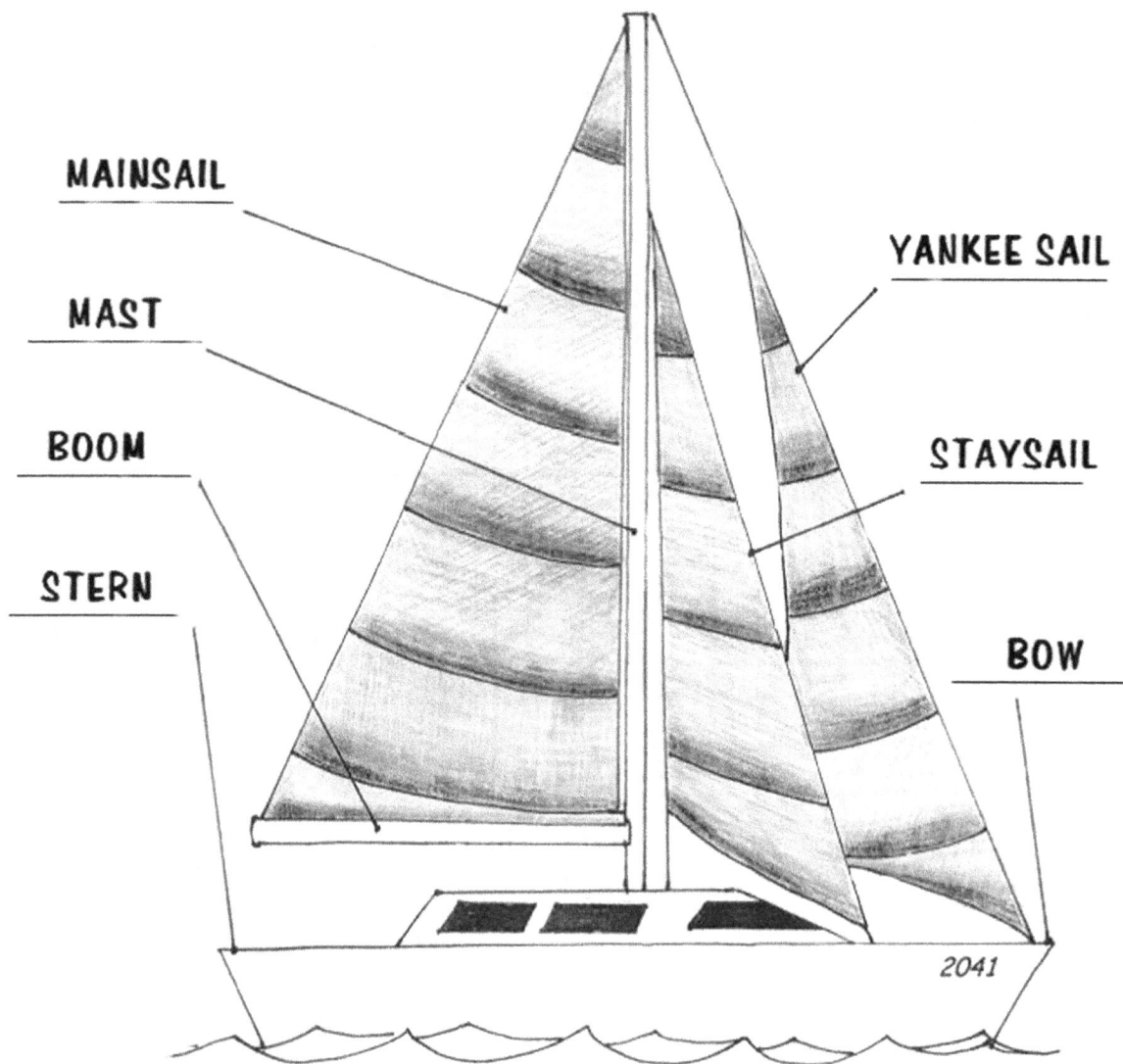

MAINSAIL

MAST

BOOM

STERN

YANKEE SAIL

STAYSAIL

BOW

2041

Appendix A

GENEROSITY WORD SCRAMBLE
ANSWER KEY

1. sharing
2. forgiving
3. mean
4. thoughtful
5. helpful
6. unselfish
7. feelings
8. caring
9. giving
10. friend

ALPHABET CODE MESSAGE
ANSWER KEY

Alphabet Code

A	B	C	D	E	F	G	H	I	J	K	L	M
1	2	3	4	5	6	7	8	9	10	11	12	13

N	O	P	Q	R	S	T	U	V	W	X	Y	Z
14	15	16	17	18	19	20	21	22	23	24	25	26

Important Message

The hard work paid off...
the cleanup by the
Russian and British team
was almost finished right
on schedule with the
stated goal of Mission
Antarctica to help clean
up Antarctica and keep it
a pristine wilderness
used only for research
and education. It showed
what could be
accomplished with
determination and effort.

Appendix A

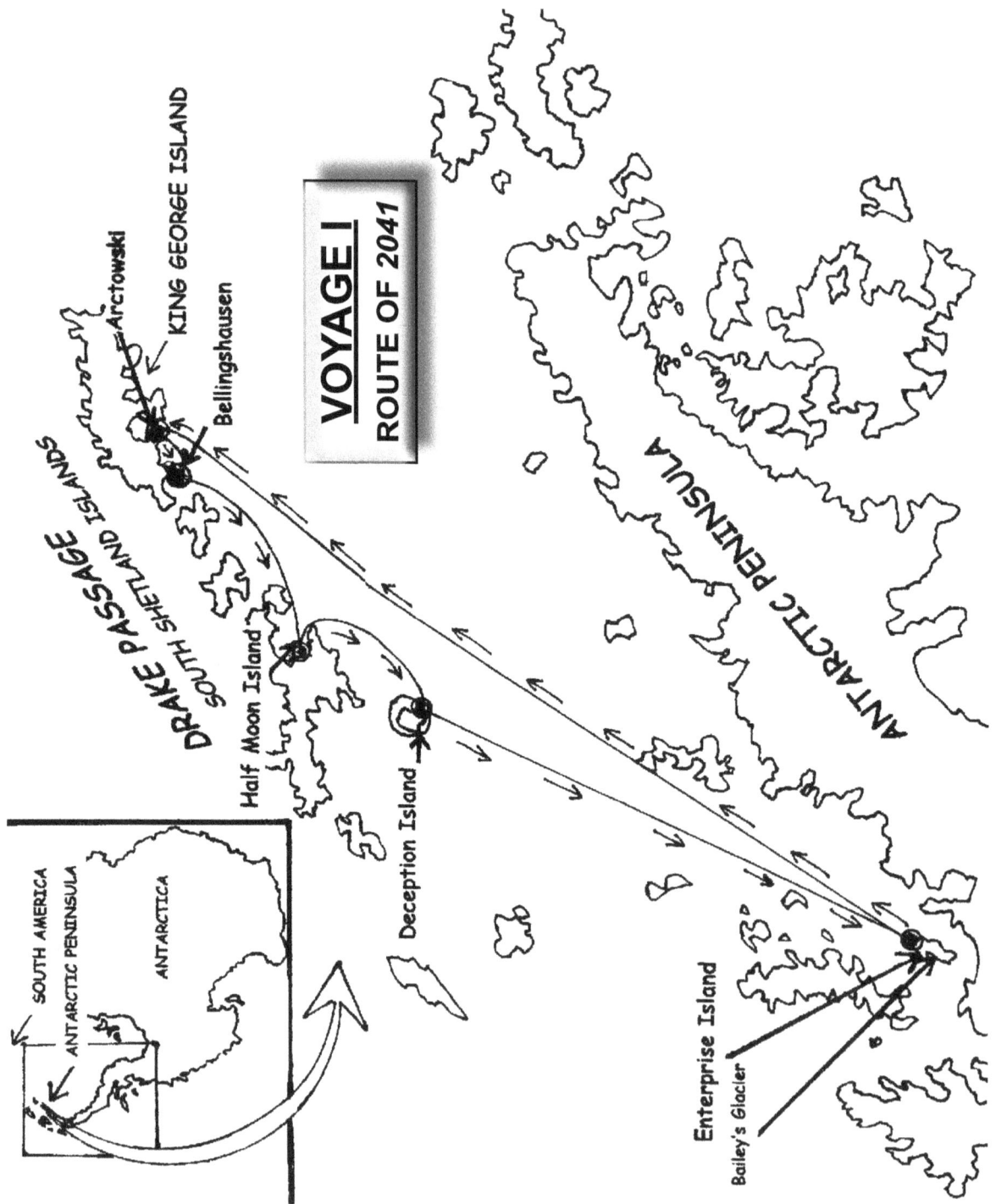

VOYAGE I
ROUTE OF 2041

KING GEORGE ISLAND
Arctowski
Bellingshausen
DRAKE PASSAGE
SOUTH SHETLAND ISLANDS
Half Moon Island
Deception Island
Enterprise Island
Bailey's Glacier
ANTARCTIC PENINSULA

SOUTH AMERICA
ANTARCTIC PENINSULA
ANTARCTICA

Appendix B

MISSION ANTARCTICA / INSPIA!
TIMELINE

1986-1989
Robert Swan becomes the first person to walk to both the North and South poles on foot. He experiences the effects of global warming at both locations

1992-1996
Robert Swan is keynote speaker at the Earth Summit in Rio de Janiero. He is awarded the Order of the British Empire by Queen Elisabeth II. Mission Antarctica is born.

1994
Robert Swan becomes Special Envoy to the Director General of UNESCO.

1997
"One Step Beyond" expedition decides that Mission Antarctica should assist the Russians in removing over 1000 tons of waste from their Bellingshausen base on King George Island on the tip of the Antarctic Peninsula.

1998-2001
Environmental and waste management experts visit Bellingshausen. Preparation for waste removal is begun. Yacht *2041* is purchased. A teacher's team arrives at Bellingshausen and the educational outreach program begins.

2001-2002
Clean-up vessel *Anne Boye* arrives in Antarctica. The waste is removed in one of the most extraordinary clean-up operations in Antarctic history. Waste is shipped to Montevideo, Uruguay where it is successfully recycled.

2002
Sponsored teachers, students and employees embark on a number of voyages aboard *2041*. They assist with the cleanup and sail around the pristine Antarctic Peninsula. Mission Antarctica and loveLife join forces.

April 2002
After sailing around the Antarctic Peninsula, the loveLife groundBREAKERS return triumphantly to South Africa. *2041* is taken out of the water and begins an historic overland journey on its way to the World Summit on Sustainable Development in Johannesburg in August 2002.

May-August 2002
The groundBREAKERS visit numerous cities and townships, meeting with local authorities and educating the community on AIDS awareness and environmental responsibility. Earthship Mission Possible in partnership with the loveLife convoy arrives in Johannesburg.

August 2002
Over 35,000 people visit the Mission Antarctica Ice Station Johannesburg site at the World Summit. Robert Swan reports to numerous Heads of State, United Nations officials and dignitaries. School children, young students and thousands of visitors pledge their support for Mission Antarctica.

September 2002
Ice Station Johannesburg wins the Best Overall Contribution to the Ubuntu Village at the World Summit. Mission Antarctica and Robert Swan announce plans for the future and launch a new name: INSPIA!

Appendix C

October-November 2002
2041 is refitted and Inspia! joins forces with Coca-Cola for the Capetown to Rio Race.

2002-2007
Robert Swan's dream of building the world's first educational base (E-Base) in Antarctica becomes a reality.

February 2003
Inspia! *2041* arrives in Rio de Janiero. Robert Swan and the Inspia! team continue to communicate a powerful message to organizations across the globe about personal leadership, teamwork and environmental responsibility.

2007
Antarctic Youth Ambassador Programme is launched in association with the Antarctica New Zealand and the Antarctic Heritage Trust.

2008
Powered entirely off renewable energy, Robert Swan and a small team live in Antarctica and broadcast to schools and universities demonstrating clean technology and energy saving techniques.

Spring 2010
In partnership with China Light and Power, a small team live at the E-Base and repair damages to the 'Live 365' equipment so that the E-Base can continue to broadcast.

2010
The Trust is engaged in a long-term cold conservation project to protect the explorers' legacy: the bases and the artifacts they left behind for current and future generations.

March 2014
GEMS Modern Academy becomes the first school to join Robert Swan's mission to save Antarctica. The group, Leadership in the Edge, sets off for Antarctica to test their leadership skills

2014
The 50 Antarctic Treaty nations represent about two-thirds of the world's human population.

July 4, 2014
The Launch of the New World, South Pole Energy Challenge, takes place.

September 23, 2014
A week-long United Nations Climate Summit begins in New York City. This summit differs from others with an unprecedented number of companies, investors, and finance ministers joining heads of state and environmentalists at one of the largest gatherings ever on climate change.

March 2015
United States President Barack Obama orders the federal government to cut its emissions of greenhouse gases by 40 percent.

2015
The International Antarctic Expedition (IAE 2015) takes a carefully selected team of corporate leaders, environmentalists, entrepreneurs, teachers, and young people on an expedition.

Appendix C

(TIMELINE continued)

April 2015
As Chair of the Arctic Council, John Kerry, United States Secretary of State, pushes for a decrease in greenhouse-gas emissions by cities, universities, and other institutions, as well as increased citizen support in reducing carbon pollution blamed for the planet's warming.

September 2015
Pope Francis, in his White House speech, addresses the issue of climate change, stating it can no longer be left to future generations.

November 30 - December 12, 2015 The Paris COP21 agreement on climate change is signed by 196 developed and developing countries, a historic, durable, and ambitious deal.

November 2015 – January 2016 Robert Swan leads 'The Return from the South Pole,' an expedition retracing his steps 30 years before.

KRILL: THE ANTARCTICA FOOD CHAIN

The word **krill** is of Norwegian origin and means very small fish, or whale food. There are some 85 species of these shrimp-like crustaceans; 11 of these are found only in Antarctic waters. The best known, and most important of these, is the largest, the two-inch-long Euphausia Superba. Antarctic krill have a life span of about five to ten years.

The Antarctic food chain is much simpler than those found in other oceans. There are fewer levels to go through from the primary producers (diatoms) to the top-level carnivores (sea birds, seals, whales, etc.). Krill feed upon phytoplankton, single-celled plants that float in the seas near the surface. In turn, krill are the primary food source for the millions of fishes, squids, penguins, albatrosses, petrels, some seals, and large baleen whales that inhabit the Southern Ocean. In fact, virtually all of the animals that visitors encounter in Antarctica are completely dependent upon the vast populations of krill for their livelihood, either directly or indirectly.

Krill and other zooplankton are being destroyed by increased levels of Ultraviolet B radiation due to global warming. Without krill, there are no whales, no penguins, no seals, no birds. Already, some penguin populations on Antarctic islands have been reduced by up to 50 percent. Krill are absolutely essential to the whole Antarctic food chain. The krill population could possibly return if the warming is no more than a climatic fluctuation, and temperatures cool. Otherwise, in less than 20 years, the Antarctic peninsula region could be very different than it is today.

Bibliography:
www.yahoo.com (Search: Krill - Antarctic Food Chain)

#5 Ozone, Global Warming: Krill and the Circle of Life

#6 CNN - Antarctic Krill Population Decreasing - July 6, 1997

www.yahoo.com (Search: Enchanted Learning Softward - Krill Printout)

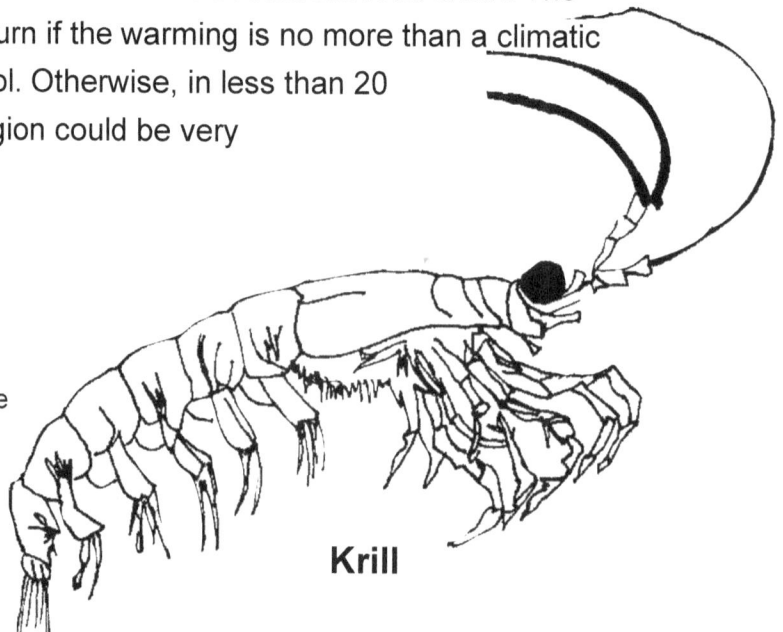

Krill

Appendix D

RECOMMENDED READING/WEBSITES

ADULTS

Cherry-Garrard, Apsley. *Worst Journey in the World.* (London: Constable, 1922)

Collier,Graham and Patricia. *Antarctic Odyssey.* (New York: Carroll & Graf Publishers, Inc., 1999)

Huntford, Roland. *The Last Place on Earth.* (London: Hodder & Stoughton, 1979)

Lansing, Alfred. *Endurance.* (London: Hodder & Stoughton, 1959)

Lonely Planet. *Antarctica.* (Victoria: Lonely Planet Publications, 2000)

Mear, Roger and Swan, Robert. *In The Footsteps of Scott.* (London: Jonathan Cape, 1987)

Reader's Digest. *Antarctica: The Extraordinary History of Man's Conquest of the Frozen Continent.* (Sydney: Reader's Digest, 1990)

Scott, Captain Robert F. *Scott's Last Expedition.* (London: Smith, Elder & Co., 1913)

Swan, Robert with Gil Reavill. *The Earth's Last Wilderness – A Quest to Save Antarctica.* (New York: Broadway Books, 2009)

Shackleton, Ernest. *South.* (London: Trafalgar Square, 1992)

Walsh, Bryan with *TIME* correspondents. *Global Warming – The Causes, The Perils, The Solutions.* (New York: TIME Books, 2012)

Wheeler, Sarah. *Terra Incognita.* (New York: The Modern Library, 1996)

CHILDREN/ADOLESCENTS

Antarctica Discovery Library. *(Series).* (Vero Beach, FL: Rourke Publishing, 1995)

Cowcher, Helen. *Antarctica.* (New York: Farrar, Straus & Giroux, 1990)

Darling, Louis. *Penguins.* (London: Angus & Robertson, 1961)

Fothergill, Alastair. *Life in the Freezer.* (London: BBC Children's Books, 1994)

Appendix E

Hooper, Meredith. *A for Antarctica.* (London: Pan Books, 1991)

Hooper, Meredith. *Tom's Rabbit.* (London: Frances Lincoln, 1998)

Lester, Alison. *Ernie Dances to the Didgeridoo.* (Sydney: Hodder Headline Australia Pty Limited, 2001)

McCurdy, Michael. *Shackleton's Amazing Antarctic Adventure: Trapped by the Ice!* (New York: Walker & Co., 1997)

Williams, Geoffrey T. *The Last Frontier: Antarctica.* (Los Angeles: Price, Stern, Sloan,1992)

WEBSITES

www.enchantedlearning.com/school/Antarctica www.ecoscope.com/krill

www.gdargaud.net/Antarctica/Index.html

www.google.com

    Search: "Antarctic Peninsula"

    Search: "Antarctica - Children

www.inspia.org

www.yahoo.com

    Search: Enchanted Learning Software - Krill Printout Search: Krill - Antarctic Food Chain Search: Penguins - Birds

www.zoobooks.com

www.zoobooks.com/animalsAtoZ/penguins.html

hppt://2041.com (2041 Foundation)

www.ingramcontent.com/pod-product-compliance
Lightning Source LLC
Chambersburg PA
CBHW081150270326
41930CB00014B/3096